For my dad, you will forever be my hero x

Please be aware that I've kindly protected all names and identifying details by disguising them. No offence intended.

Contents

FYI, before you continue to read, just in case you have purchased this book with the expectations of perfection… you won't find it.

This book may not have been penned by an author, sitting at an immaculate desk, on their expensive MacBook with their beautifully manicured fingers, typing each word with grace and presence, nope… I'm sorry to disappoint, this is just me.

I left school at the tender age of sixteen, with the grades of every letter of the alphabet, (well all except A).

Instead, I'm surrounded by dog eared notebooks and scraps of paper, typing on a small mobile phone screen, because half the time I can't even find the iPad, since a certain little person has stolen it to play Roblox on!

However, what I can tell you is every word, sentence and paragraph is manuscript with honesty, love and all the strength I have within my soul. (Oh, and a bucket full of coffee)

Most of all, it's written from the bottom of my heart, so please... be kind.

This book is dedicated to those who are fighting against mental illness, and to the survivors of abuse.

Always believe that there is hope and never lose sight of who you are.

To my closest family and friends, who there are too many to mention individually. They are the ones who know me inside out and believe in me. (You know who you special people are because I'm always telling you), Thank you for supporting me with your love and honesty, I will be forever grateful.

To my baby bears, my three little angels, I couldn't be prouder of you. My only wish is that you take the path that brings you the most happiness. Thank you for teaching me the true meaning and the precious gift of love. You three are the reason I wake in the morning.

Everything I do, I do for you. My love for you is unconditional and never ending.

And last but no means least, my very own 007. Thank you for staying loyal, honest, and teaching me how to be strong in this troublesome world by facing it head on. Thank you most of all for being the best daddy to our cubs. You are their world.

I love you all, for always and always xx

A note with love from me to you beautiful people out there,

For years it's only ever been my dream to author this book, searching for the right words while trying to overcome my self-doubt, waiting for any signs or guidance, until I found the courage, strength, and confidence to believe in myself.

This is my time to tell MY story...
So here I'm sharing with you the events of my life, how I have learnt to deal with the past and how I have found the strength to carry on no matter what life has thrown at me.

My only hope is that it can bring comfort, love, and support to those who need it, and that what I share will give other survivors the confidence to find their own voice to speak out and stop abusers ruining lives.

If at the end of this I've helped just one lost soul, then I'll feel that revisiting a painful time in my past has been worth all the pain and the tears.

Always remember you are special, and you deserve every happiness in your life.

Always try to make everyone feel like a someone.

Always take care of yourself first.

Always believe in your dreams.

Always make them happen and … don't you EVER give up.

With love xxx

Prologue

"I'm Mandy and you're Sharon," I said to my little sister Hollie as we played mums and babies together. Why we called each other that I'll never know, but for some weird reason the names just stuck, (the same as our babies were always Cherrie-Adele and Christopher.) Hollie wasn't just my sister, she was also my best friend, and as her big sister I felt a great protection for her. We were partners in crime but in a funny, cheeky, and cute kind of way. Together we made a promise, that we'd always

be there for each other. I've all kinds of beautiful memories of our times together, that I'll hold on to forever…

I grew up in a large family, in a quiet village. My Mam Roxanne and my Dad William, (everyone called him Bill), lived by strong

Christian morals. We were educated from a very young age that *'manners don't cost anything.'* We taught to never lie, no matter how much trouble we thought we would be in. And most importantly we must always be kind and helpful to others. Before every meal we would take it in turns to say grace, "*For what we are about to receive may the lord make us truly thankful.*" Throughout my childhood I learnt to be grateful for everything I had.

I was born in December of 1983, then two years later my sister Hollie arrived. Although we were very close, we were completely the opposite of each other. Hollie was taller than me, so everyone thought I was the younger sister. I had light straight hair and she had curly dark hair. Hollie was quiet, whereas I liked to sing and dance all the time, (although it wouldn't take much to persuade her to join in with my 'shows' I put on for the family). When I was nine years old, our baby brother Harry was born, with his white, blonde curly locks of hair. Both my Mam and Dad had children from previous marriages, not that it made any difference, because I was as evenly close to them. My Aunty Jenny is my God Mother and is also my dad's previous wife. I loved spending time with her and my older brother Leo and sister Eden. I'm just glad Aunty Jenny forgave me after the day she took us to the park, pushed me on the swing and I accidentally kicked her in the mouth, making it bleed. We would '*Boo and Hiss*' at the pantos we went to watch at the theatre together, and she would take us swimming once a month. Aunty Jenny was a special part of my life, and she always will be.

The music that filled our house were the best memories that I keep from my childhood. Mum listened to the '*Beach Boys*' and '*The Hollies,*' and Dad had a massive collection of records and tapes of just about every era you could imagine. I loved it when Dad played his guitar, me and Hollie would dance around the house to *Status Quo* '*Rocking all over the world.*' I was at my happiest when I'd sit on my dad's lap and we'd sing, '*In the army now,*' together. I'll never forget my first ever Walkman they bought me, I thought I was so cool as I bopped my head around to the beat of the music, it came everywhere with me. My first cassette tape was a mix of artists from the seventies, I'd sing along to "*Rose Garden*' and '*All the young dudes.*' I could escape the world and even if it was only for a while, it felt bliss. Even now when I'm feeling low, I have a playlist on my phone called '*Mam & Dads.*' It's a mix of songs from the past, I just put my headphones on…grab my favourite Cath Kidston pen… and write.

Like me, Dad loved to help others, which is why he was so good at his work. He was a firefighter and a mechanic, often looking at friends' cars in exchange for a packet of twenty '*Benson & Hedges.*'
He was a proper 'fixer.' In almost any crisis Dad's motto was always, "*Stick kettle on lovey,*

let's have a brew," I think this will forever be my coping strategy, as simple as it may sound, it helps. I felt so thankful to have such a hardworking Dad, because life had never been easy for him. My heart would hurt for him and everything he'd missed over the years. Dad's Mam passed away when he was only thirteen, and his dad when he was in his early twenties, so sadly we never had the chance to meet them. He did have a step mam we called Grandma Lilah; she had a pet canary bird called Amber who lived in her front room in a big gold cage. Grandma Lilah loved birds, she had a big poster full of several types on the back of her kitchen door and would teach us all about them. Just before we went home, she'd ask us to open our hand and she'd give us each a gold shiny coin. I remember feeling sad when we had to leave her, because I didn't like to think that she was all on her own.

Dad was always telling us funny stories from when he was a boy, proudly he'd show us all his old photographs of his family, with a story behind each one. I loved the way I could sit for hours with him and cherish the memories he had made when he was younger, with his friends and his older sisters. I was close to both my Aunties but they like the rest of our family still lived up North, so we only got to see them a few times a year. I'd imagine they were grateful for this, as I would spend the whole time brushing their hair and painting on make up while jabbering on in their ear holes. It would make me smile so much when Dad said that I reminded him of his mum, because she was dainty with small feet like mine.

I couldn't have felt prouder of him and all that he had gone on to achieve in life, even if he did convince me that if I kept digging in the patch of mud in the garden I'd end up in Australia. I'd picture in my head Kylie Minogue and Jason Donovan greeting me off the plane, with sweat dripping off my brow as I dug with my red plastic spade for hours.

When we were little Dad was very busy with shift work, which we found hard at times like birthdays and Christmas, we had to make the most out of our time together when he was at home. Although they can laugh about it now, it wasn't funny at the time when Dad ran out on a call. Mam had taken me up to bed when suddenly the fire alarm started sounding off. Dad had been boiling a pan of milk on the hob when his bleep went. We grew used to him often jumping over tables and rushing out the door, obstacles never stopped him, for when that bleep went, he was off like a shot. There was smoke everywhere, Mam had to ring the fire brigade, slightly awkward as Dad was the driver and the alert flashed up to his own address, (even more awkward was when he realised what he had done as he turned the corner of our street and clocked my Mam's face). There we all stood outside the house freezing our butts off in our PJ's. At least we can laugh now and be thankful it wasn't any worse.

Mam would pile us all into the car and we would go shopping together, singing away to *Robson and Jerome's 'White cliffs of Dover'* on repeat at the tops of our voices. It's funny as my babies love to do the same, their favourite is the musical *'Annie,'* I smile to myself when I hear them singing their hearts out to *'Tomorrow'* in the back of the car.

Mam didn't believe in leaving us with anyone unless it was an absolute emergency, so we were very lucky that we could spend our precious early years together. To support Dad, Mam decided to start her own little candle making business from home, alongside part time childminding. It was an enormous success, but also came with its challenges, so she made the decision to dedicate her time to child minding full time instead. The house was constantly full of toys, noise, and chaos. I would forever be standing on a stickle brick or a Duplo train that had been lobbed across the room or fishing out a sock from the toilet. It was all good fun.

Mam shared a very close bond with her family, especially her Mam and Dad as they only lived around the corner from us. I loved spending time with all my Auntie's and Uncles and Cousins.

One of my most favourite places when I was growing up was my Nanna Ava and Grandpa Jack's house. They were my absolute world, and the best thing of all is that the precious memories I made with them, can never be stolen by *anyone*.

My sister and I would spend hours sitting on the lawn in Nanna and Grandpa's beautiful garden, plaiting each other's hair, making daisy chains, and laughing together. One afternoon I lay in the gorgeous sunshine, with the grass itching at my skin. I gazed up at the pure white clouds as they floated in the clear blue sky. I could hear the birds singing in the trees, it was just like I imagined heaven to be… and as I looked over at Hollie beside me, I just knew she felt it too. I wished that I could have scooped up the smells of the freshly cut grass and flowers, collecting their sweet scents into a bottle, so I could take the lid off to inhale those happy memories whenever I wanted to. I loved to go lavender picking with my Nanna, she would use it to make little pouches to keep my clothes fresh, but I preferred to keep them under my pillow to remind me of her, especially when I couldn't sleep. (I'm sure I still have one in the loft somewhere). There were two fishponds in the garden, a small, raised concrete one on the patio and another the size of a swimming pool on the grass. I loved to feed the fish and would be lost in thought, watching the tadpoles, frogs and newts playing in the water. I liked to help Grandpa water all the vegetables in the greenhouses and fruits in the vinery. It amazed me how all the fruits and vegetables would grow and then be transformed into lovely jams and puddings, and the best peach Snaps I'd ever tasted (also known as Archers). I would be allowed a tiny drop, (as Nanna called it, which was most definitely the opposite of a drop) in her special little crystal sherry glass at Christmas time, I remember my cheeks tingling as I drank it, feeling all grown up.

My most treasured place had to be right at the bottom of the garden, where there were the sweetest strawberries, raspberries and blackberries, Nanna would give me a big bowl to collect them in. Next to the rhubarb, grew my grandpa's prize sized marrows and pumpkins, he was so proud of them bless him.

In the middle of the grass was a tree where we would climb up and hide in. And this was the place we called our… *"Secret Garden."*

When it was time for tea Nanna would call us from the house, where there would be a little glass coffee table in the middle of the lounge set with plates and cutlery, real thick ham sandwiches and crisps, homemade pickles and lollipops (pickled onions to normal people) *'Bullseye'* would be playing in the background on the huge TV set in the corner of the room. I would always sit in my most loved place, at my Nanna's feet on the white sheepskin rug. We would sing *'My bonnie lies over the ocean'* and *'Daisy Daisy'* together, as I giggled at the dramatic actions that she danced to the words.

Every couple of months we would go to visit my great Mamma Elsie and Dadda Eddie in Newcastle, (my Nanna's Mam and Dad) We didn't get to see them very often, but when we did it was like we had never been away. The table would be set just the same as at Nanna's, with thick ham and rolls and cups of tea in Mamma's special cups and saucers with pictures of blue birds on. She would wear her little pinnie tied around her waist, as she pottered around the kitchen. Dadda Eddie would sit on his brown armchair in the corner of the room, smoking his pipe. He had thick lenses in his glasses, so his eyes looked big and funny. Beside him he kept a wooden bowl of fox's glacier mints. Hollie and I would sit on his knee, and he would sing funny songs to us, our favourite was…

'Not last night but the night before, there came three tom cats at my door, one with a fiddle, one with a drum and one with a pancake on its .... bum.' We would be in stitches, just like my babies are when I sing it to them, although I'm sure mine are just laughing at me thinking that I'm as nutty as a fruitcake.

We would race laps with our cousins up and down the long garden, often ending in a scrap between me and Hollie as one accused the other one of cheating. The only thing I didn't like was the outside toilet, it was freezing cold with cobwebs everywhere, so I'd keep my legs crossed for as long as I could.

I longed for those days to last forever, I felt so safe and loved.

It wouldn't be long before we'd be gathered again at Christmas time or special occasions with all the family together at Nanna Ava and

Grandpa Jack's house. Although I loved Christmas, I always felt so overwhelmed and emotional at the same time. In between my tears I would play with my cousins in the 'Music room,' while the grownups would drink booze and sleep in the lounge or play with our Christmas presents, we had taken with us, especially my dad and Uncle Jay, they were such big kids!

I think you may be able to gather by now, that my family were very musical, Grandpa played the organ and piano as did my Mam and my Uncle Joe. My Uncle Jay played the trombone. In the corner of the room there was a basket full of instruments for us to play with like, maracas, bells, and a tambourine. I was always last to choose, so inevitably I'd end up with the crappy triangle, then basically we'd make as much noise as we possibly could, rolling around, laughing so much that our bellies hurt.

Memories were created enjoying holidays together too; my heart would jump excitedly when Nanna Ava asked me if I'd like to go to the seaside. We'd suck on boiled sweets out of the little gold tin she kept in the car door, while listening to her Patsy Cline cassette tape play in her bright blue fiesta, which I found so funny as it had the word *"Fashion"* printed on the side of it in pink fancy writing. Nanna just didn't care what anyone thought, and I loved that about her.

One weekend we were travelling up the motorway when we went past a speed camera that flashed,

"Well," she said, *"I'm not going as fast as them in front of us"*, I was dying with laughter, you just

couldn't help it, as we approached the traffic light at the roundabout, she passes straight through the red light, *"Erm, do you think I should go back?"*, she asks, I was howling…

Yep, that's where I get it from for sure.

We would stay in their little caravan, which was situated on an immaculate park in Somerset. Hollie and I would make our own entertainment by rolling down green grassy banks or walking to the beach and shops for ice cream. I'd dread it if it were the SPAR shop though because Nanna would make sure the shop assistant was fully aware of the fact that she thought everything was ultra-expensive.

She'd huff and puff at the checkout, *"Well, it's not that dear in Sainsburys,"* she'd exclaim, reluctantly handing her money over. She wasn't overly impressed with the pick n mix in woollies either, ordering us to empty the contents of the paper bag back into the plastic stand. She was so funny.

"Try this skirt on, you need to make sure it fits you," she would say in the shop which looked like a jumble sale, with no such thing as a dressing room in sight. I would blush with embarrassment, *"But Nanna, there's nowhere to go,"* I'd whisper. She would then take off her long beige mac and hold it up in front of me. There I'd be, crouched down half naked in the corner of the shop, surrounded by a pile of clothes, (I probably didn't like, but she thought they looked wonderful.) Although I wouldn't argue with her, because she had a funny way of persuading me to do just about anything.) Nanna Ava's pet hate was if you didn't wear a coat that covered your arse, and she would make sure you knew it. *"Oh, you'll get such a cold*

bum" she'd shout. You can imagine she wasn't impressed one bit when I proudly strolled in with my new 'Spliffy' jacket on, (that I'd persuaded Dad to buy me off the Market.) I thought I was going to have to pick her jaw up off the floor when she clocked on to what it meant. Once She had picked her jaw up, she'd say, *"Take your coat off duck or you won't feel benefit,"* (not bad grammar by the way, that's just how she said it, she never pronounced 'the') I'd never know if I was coming or going!

Hollie and I would skip into the arcades, with the sand off the beach continuing to scratch and exfoliate our feet. Wearing our matching pink jelly shoes, armed with our two pence coins, that we'd been saving like forever. The only complaint I ever had, was the food (sorry Nanna but it was just the worst,) we'd sit and eat at a little fold up table in the awning of the caravan. On the menu would be *always* … Tinned mince, tinned potatoes, and tinned process peas (wuuuurp), if we didn't eat it there would be no pudding. I didn't eat at the best of times, so it was kind of torture when Nanna would dish it out on to the melamine plate in front of me. The truth was, I knew that Nanna kept most tins past there consumption date, and I mean as in years out, *"Ah, it wunt hurt you"* she'd laugh in her lovely northern accent. When we weren't spending time with my grandparents, we'd be at our static caravan in Wales. In fact, majority of our school holidays we'd spend travelling back and forth down the motorway in the middle of the night. We tended to spend more time with our friends up there than we did at home. When we returned to school after the summer break with our Liverpudlian accents our friends would think it was hilarious.

It's all those happy memories that I didn't even appreciate we were making that have kept me going and given me the strength to carry on. Often, I close my eyes and dream of being back there, living my best life.

Children learn what they live - Dorothy Law Nolte (1924 -2005)

If a child lives with criticism, they learn to condemn.

If a child lives with hostility, they learn to fight.

If a child lives with fear, they learn to be apprehensive.

If a child lives with pity, they learn to feel sorry for themselves.

If a child lives with jealousy, they learn to envy.

If a child lives with shame, they learn to feel guilty.

If a child lives with encouragement, they learn confidence.

If a child lives with tolerance, they learn patience.

If a child lives with praise, they learn appreciation.

If a child lives with acceptance, they learn to love.

If a child lives with approval, they learn to like themselves.

If a child lives with recognition, they learn it is good to have a goal.

If a child lives with sharing, they learn generosity.

If a child lives with honesty, they learn truthfulness.

If a child lives with fairness, they learn justice.

If a child lives with kindness and consideration, they learn respect.

If a child lives with security, they learn to have faith in themselves and in those about them.

If a child lives with friendliness, they learn the world is
a wonderful place in which we live.

Rose-tinted specs

I was about seven years old when I first found
my love for writing. It was far easier and more
powerful way, to release my thoughts and
feelings down on paper, rather than speaking
aloud. The more I could express myself, the

stronger I felt that something had awakened within me…

I was in junior school when I thought up my first story, titled, '*A journey through space.*' I spent hours brainstorming loads of exciting ideas on sheets of A4 paper. I was so proud of this little creation I'd made up by myself, especially because I knew nothing about space, it was solely based on my imagination. My next story was invented when I was at high school. God only knows what Ms Merrill, my English teacher thought when I excitedly presented her with a twenty-six-page essay that I'd made up about a slug… named Sebastian Stallone. Oh, he was such a happy little guy, he spent hours sitting on a beach on his deckchair. He even had a mobile phone. (Don't judge). All I do know is that my story was handed around the staff room, although I was never sure if that was a good sign or a bad one.

Strangely, I felt the need to write letters and notes to just about everyone. Mam would often be enjoying a nice soak in peace, when a note would slide under the bathroom door.

'Sorry mam I know you're in the bath, but I really, really, want a biscuit can I have one please, please, please? Tick Y for yes and N for no in the boxes thank you. PS, please say yes'

One afternoon after being bollocked by Mam and dad for putting too much sugar in Harry's tommee tipee cup, (I tipped in half the jar, who even uses a spoon anyway.) Sulking my mardy arse off into the back garden, stomping through the kitchen I grabbed a pen, piece of paper and a little fisher price doll and shoved them in the pocket of my dungarees. I sat on the grass inside our little playhouse made from 'For Sale' sign boards and wrote a note. I then stuck it up the dolls bottom, and chucked it over next doors garden, it read…

If you find me, I'm very sad, please help, PS throw me back over the wall thank you, BIG loves.'

Throughout my teenage years, I'd send letters to my friends if they were upset to reassure them that I was never far away. I'd scribble notes to my boyfriend's declaring my undying love for them, (cringe). I would always end my letters in the same way, *'I'm always here to share the tears, the fears, the smiles and the laughter.'*

So yeah, I was proper deep, even then.

The letters then led to me writing daily diary entries and journals, allowing me to let go of my thoughts. This is how my journey to recovery began…

Nine years ago, I sat and wrote a letter to *him*, to Nathan.

A letter that uncovered a whole past of pain and hurt. But at last, I'd done it, I'd found the courage to confront him. I wanted him to realise just what an impact his actions had had on my life, leaving me with pain and trauma.

I saw the best in everyone and trusted that I was surrounded by those who loved me, until one day I discovered that 'Trust' had no meaning. It'd been snatched away from me and ripped into shreds. It wasn't until I had children of my own, that I felt an overwhelming love and protection for them. I realised that living in fear was far from okay.

The biggest battle I came to fight, was learning to let go of the shame, guilt and blame that had consumed me for so long. I didn't want to be at war with these negative emotions that weighed me down. My body was exhausted, and I ached from all the tears that I'd shed in secret. My head thumped like a never-ending migraine, while flashbacks of the past replayed over and over in my mind. It was time to put the past and the years of addiction and self-harm behind me, but more importantly it was time to say goodbye to that sad, frightened little girl …

 We lived in an old, detached Victorian house in a quiet little village. Entering the front door was a long narrow hallway which led into a large front room. In the corner of the room was a brown wooden door, behind it was a flight of concrete steps leading down into a cold, dark cellar. Dads' newspaper collection was stacked floor to ceiling, God only knows how many years back they dated. He was forever collecting things. He'd all sorts of memorabilia, there were piles of records, stamps and even a shed full of glass milk bottles, (that's right a whole shed). I remember us sitting together at the breakfast table one morning, as he turned to me and said, "*When you're a big girl the milk won't come like this anymore in these glass bottles, nope it will be in plastic cartons in the shops, and that's why I have to save them.*" I'd laugh at the excuses he gave mam, as he defended the crap he held onto, refusing to throw anything away.

I'd avoid the cellar room at all costs, it was way too creepy for me, except for the time Dad and Nathan set up a big train set down there. I slowly crept down one step at a time into the cold dark room, I watched the trains race around the track, though it wasn't long before I was yawning and fidgeting with boredom. The smell of damp lingered from the well below. It didn't help that someone had once told me that a lady had died down there, so I was petrified. My hamstrings had a rude awakening as I raced back up them concrete steps as quick as my little legs would carry me, jumping two steps at a time, crapping myself at the thought of someone chasing me.

I was such a scaredy cat, and I was convinced the upstairs of the house was haunted, because both my sister and I had described the same tall lady, standing at the end of the landing next to the bathroom. She had long dark hair and wore a white old-fashioned nightdress, the very same one you see in all the horror films, it was weird as we just grew used to her presence.

At the top of the stairs to the left, situated at the front of the house was my Mam and Dad's bedroom, to the right of the stairs there was a long landing, with my brother Nathan's bedroom at the far end, next to the bathroom. Hollie and I shared the middle bedroom, with our old rickety wooden bunkbeds that creaked every time we rolled over. I had a white flowery *forever friends* duvet set on my bed; Hollie had a pink polka dot one on hers with a dog on it called *scruff*. At the bottom of our beds sat our huge identical teddy panda bears.

Just outside our bedroom door was a loose piece of carpet, covering a wonky floorboard where the heating pipes ran. I lifted it up one day and made a little house for the *'Borrower's family.'* (A family of little people who had nowhere to live, they would squirrel away food and treasures like buttons when everyone was asleep, or out of the house). I carefully decorated it, making all sorts of bits of furniture and pretty things for them. At Christmas I made a little tree out of pipe cleaners and covered it with tinsel. I would dream of what the little Borrower's people would do at night when we were all sleeping. I wonder if the bits I made are still there.

When my baby brother Harry came along, Nathan moved downstairs into the extension, which my dad converted into a bedroom for him. His room was right at the back of the house, near the downstairs toilet and utility room. It was a cold, dark and unfinished room.

And this is where my nightmare ordeal first began…

I've found it hard to open up about this part of my life because it's recreated so many negative emotions.

I can still smell, I can still see, and I can still painfully feel it, even now a certain scent will turn my stomach and take me back to that cold dark room.

I was a loving and trusting child, maybe a little too trusting sometimes. My Grandpa Jack would say *"You look at the world through rose tinted spectacles me duck. Just like your mam."* I would just smile and agree as I thought it sounded nice, whatever its meaning.

I was an exceptionally sensitive soul, or should I say, *'over emotional,'* so Everyone told me, (as if it was some sort of contagious illness.) Although I found that being sensitive could be both a blessing and a curse at times.

I guess that's why Nathan chose me. He gained my trust; he took that trust and he abused it for his own gratification.

I was just eight years old, and he was a teenager.

He knew better.

I didn't.

I always thought he behaved a little odd at time's, well in fact most of the time, but I just accepted he was my brother and that was okay.

I was playing with my barbie dolls on the living room floor. Nala my cat rolled around by my side as the warm sun shone through the window, she was never far away. He caught my eye as he lingered in the living room doorway, beckoning me to go into the kitchen. Assuming he was just preparing one of his weird combos of jam and peanut butter sarnies, I went with him. Completely unaware of what was about to happen. I walked into the kitchen when he continued towards his bedroom, I thought it was strange, but I followed, '*Maybe he wants to show me that his snakes shed its skin again,*' I thought to myself innocently. But it wasn't that either.

Leading me into the toilet, he whispered for me to "*shush*," closing the door quietly behind him Anxiously I stood there, froze to the spot. From the fluttering in my belly, I knew something wasn't right. My heart began pounding so hard through my little chest that I could feel the vibration in my throat. Tension passed through my whole body as I tried my hardest not to look at him in the face. I looked down at my pink *my little pony* pants as they fell to the floor. He started touching me in places, I knew felt wrong. I was so scared that my eyes were stinging from holding back my tears. Belinda Carlisle was playing on his tape player in his bedroom next door, repeating the words in my head, *"I'm not afraid anymore,"* until it was over. Without saying a word, he calmly stood up, opened the door, and left the room as if nothing had happened. As I left the toilet my head was full of confusion and worry. I walked back into the living room and curled up on the sofa, feeling numb. I couldn't understand what had just happened, I knew it felt wrong, but I didn't know how to question it either.

I learnt that what was to be a *"Secret,"* was going to happen again. The second time was very much the same as the first, and by the third time I knew what I had to do without being coerced. The feelings were always the same, numb, frightened, and scared. Searching for something to focus on in the room when it was happening. Whether it be the buttons on the washing machine or the white paint mark on the grey bricks in the wall. I felt so confused as he'd repeatedly ask me, *"Does it feel nice?"* as if it was a mutual agreement. Did it feel nice? No, it didn't. It felt naughty and it felt bad, it made my belly ache and it hurt.

What I couldn't understand was that he didn't seem to be afraid of found out. To him it didn't matter if we were alone or if anyone else was at home. I suppose he could use the location of the toilet to his advantage though. I lived in fear, when often I'd be playing with my sister, trying my best to avoid eye contact with him when he'd make his appearance at the door. My heart would sink because I knew exactly what was coming next. I truly believed that I was to blame for what happened and I felt as though I didn't try hard enough to fight him. I never dared say no because I knew deep down, I had to do this, I had no choice, because if I didn't my sister may have been in danger, and it was my job to protect her. Always. I'd sacrifice myself for her no matter what, she'd never have to go through this, and I'd do everything in my power to prevent it.

Every morning I woke up I would pray the time before was to be the last... *"Dear God, please make it stop."* It never did though, and what was worse there was nothing I could do about it.

There was a time when I looked forward to our family holidays, but not anymore. The three of us had to share a bedroom in our static caravan. Hollie and I had a single bed each and Nathan slept in a bunk above us. I'd just be drifting off to sleep when his head or hand would appear, and he'd whisper, *"Are you awake?"* staying as still and as quiet as I could with my eyes closed tight, praying he would go to sleep. A place I had once felt safe had been robbed and I was scared. The hardest part was not being able to tell anyone, I wanted to so badly, but I couldn't find the words or the courage to do so. I was overcome by fear that

I wouldn't be believed because he too was a member of the family.

I hoped things would change when we found out Mam was expecting my baby brother, but it didn't. In fact, the year of 1992 was one of the hardest years of my life. I was just nine years old when I unexpectedly started my periods. I had no idea what was happening to me, no warning signs whatsoever. I felt so scared as I rocked back and forth on the toilet, holding my sore belly while clutching at my bloodstained knickers. My Mam came running upstairs after hearing my cries, she was as shocked and as upset as I was. There was no such thing as sex education until high school, so nothing had prepared me for this grown-up part of my life. The bleeding got heavier, and I began to experience painful cramps in my stomach. Mam briefly explained to me what was happening to my body, she gave me one of her massive sanitary towels, I must have looked like I had a cucumber stuck up my arse as I waddled to the chemist with her. We went over to the sanitary section, and she let me choose some more comfortable ones, and just like that… I was a 'lady.'

Life was then completely over shadowed when my Grandpa Jack was diagnosed with cancer. He'd been suffering with stomach pains for a while, but unlike when he gave me a mug of hot water with a drop of brandy and sugar in it to help my belly aches, it didn't help his. I think I must have inherited my nerves from my grandpa, he too was a worrier. Life hadn't always been easy for him though bless his heart. Grandpa Jack was only a baby when he was adopted. He didn't really talk to me about that part of his life, and I didn't want to pry, but it would explain why he was anxious.

Grandpa was a genuinely lovely man; he was a friend to everyone, and he loved his family so much. I guess you could say he was the glue holding us all together. Nanna and Grandpa were so close, I hoped that one day I would find someone special to share the love that they had for each other. No amount of money could ever buy that.

They had been busy making so many plans for their future retirement together. They had bought a lovely new touring caravan, and Grandpa had built a beautiful summer house in his beloved garden. He found the energy to walk and sit in it just once, after it was finished.

I'd reminisce with him about our happy memories together as I couldn't understand why he could no longer race us up and down the garden in his barrow… just one last time.

Six weeks before, I watched him walk through them conservatory doors, wearing his long grey coat, carrying his briefcase. He made me laugh until I cried, and now here I sat beside him, with tears streaming down my face, with the Marie curie nurses gently explaining to us that although he couldn't see us, he could still hear our voices. I gazed up at my Grampa, who I loved so very much, wishing it were all a dream, while praying he would open his eyes just one last time and say, *"There, there, don't cry me duck, I'll be okay."*

Grandpa was deteriorating rapidly, and he looked so thin and frail. He had a stomach bag because he could no longer use the toilet, which would make funny growling noises, we thought it was alive, so we named it 'George.'

Grampa fought on until my brother Harry arrived, I'm sure he held on to have that precious cuddle with him. Three weeks later, on a scorching day in august, he took his last breath with my Nanna at his side. My heart was shattered because of how cruelly he'd been taken from us. I'd spend so much time in the garden just to feel close to him., talking to him in the hope that he could somehow hear me.

One night the most surreal thing happened to me, after spending the day in Grandpa Jacks Garden. I was fast asleep when I suddenly woke, struggling to catch my breath, as if I were underwater. Sweat was dripping down my forehead when I heard my grandpa's voice so clearly calling my name. I rubbed by eyes in disbelief, looking up, I saw a bright light surrounding my grandpa's face. There he was as clear as a picture looking towards me. He had so much love and peace in his eyes, whether it was a dream or not it felt real to me. I knew it was his way of reassuring me that he was ok.

Nanna Ava was like my best friend, she was always there for me, not once did she ever let me down, and all the strength I had was because of her. It was now my turn to be there for her. We would spend hours together chatting away, or should I say, 'I,' would spend hours chatting away, she would just listen and nod off here and there, I'm sure she thought I rambled on way too much. She always laughed at the crazy stories I told her though. Nanna told me that I should have been a comedian, although I didn't know what one was, until I watched Peter Kay on video tape when I went to stay with my Uncle Jay and Aunty Lissa in Newcastle.

Sleep overs were the best at Nanna's, it was our special time, just me and her. We would stay up until eleven o' clock watching movies together, our favourite was *National Velvet.'* It was a lovely old film about a young girl called velvet, she desperately wanted to win a horse called 'The Pie,' in a raffle. Her dream comes true and together they go on to win the Grand National. Nanna even taped it for me so I could watch it at home, bless her. The last movie we ever watched together was *'Titanic.'* I still can't watch it all the way through without crying. When the adverts came on the telly, Nanna would disappear off upstairs to turn our electric blankets on, so the beds were nice and warm before we got in them. I would then have the best night's sleep ever, I felt so safe in the warm and comfortable double bed my Nanna had prepared, just for me. I loved the feel of the crisp freshly washed and neatly pressed sheets against my skin. I'd snuggle up in the blankets that smelt of her washing powder and drift off to sleep, smiling to myself as I looked at the little white teas made on the bedside table, all ready for the morning brew. (I'd love one of them now). Nanna spoiled me with her love, every minute with her was special and I was so grateful to her for helping me escape from what was happening at home.

Life was challenging with a new baby in the house, but I never minded helping with the chores, going to the shops, and playing mam to my little brother. We were all still grieving for Grandpa, especially my Mam. I'd do whatever I could to ease things for her, despite knowing that the pain of her grief wasn't going to be relieved easily.

Amongst all the stress that surrounded our family, I continued to suffer in silence. Every day I'd open my eyes and ask myself the same questions, *"Why? "Why is this happening to me?" "What did I do?" Or "What didn't I do?"* listening for the answers that never came.

In the year of 1997, we moved to a new house in a different area. Our new home was much smaller, which made the abuse difficult to persist, and eventually it stopped. Well, physically it had anyway. When Nathan was around the house, I would try to stay out of his way. I avoided looking at him or talking to him because I would feel so uncomfortable, sensing him watching me over his glasses.

After a while, Nathan moved in with my Nanna Ava. Living in a smaller house was proving to be difficult, testosterone was flying about between him and my dad, which led to lots of intense arguments. Although I would visit her as often as I could, I didn't feel I was able to stay with her anymore. I'd been robbed of another place that I had once felt safe and happy. No matter what happened though I'd never let him come between Nanna and me, our bond was too strong for that.

Even with Nathan gone, I struggled to move on. I tried my hardest to block out the sad memories and save myself from the pain. The thing is though, when your 'over emotional,' it's not as easy as that, especially when there are moments that will continue to awaken feelings of sadness and loneliness. I'd gone from being an affectionate child with so much love to give, to being a shadow of my former self, wanting to hide away from the world. I couldn't bear physical touch anymore, wincing if I had to kiss or cuddle family and friends when they came to visit. If I saw Mam and Dad showing affection of any kind, it would make me feel physically sick. Inside I would be screaming over something that seemed so natural to others. It sounds pathetic I know, and I hated what was happening to me, because I knew it wasn't normal. What hurt the most was that I wanted to be like other children, in other families. Their lives were so perfect, and although I'd never feel envious of what they had, I did wish that I could trade lives with them, even for a moment.

It wasn't just the physical side of the abuse that had affected me because it went much deeper than that. When leaving his pornography in places where he knew I couldn't help but see it was just another way of abusing me without touching me. I can't just unsee the images I saw at such a young age, if only it was that simple to erase them. I will say that I'll never allow my children to witness such material in my house. I hate porn of any kind or anything relating to it. It brings back too many painful memories of my past when all I want to do is just forget it all … the pornography…the abuse…the staring… *everything.*

Unless a person has felt that pain, which I pray to God they don't, and my heart goes out deeply to you if you have. No one can possibly judge or understand the way I think, how I act, why my emotions are so up and down like a yoyo, and how a simple word can change my mood instantly.

It then occurred to me, just what Grampa meant when he said that I looked at the world through 'rose tinted specs.'

The world wasn't rosy one bit though, was it? it was full of terrible, tragic things which happened every day, even if there was such a beautiful paradise called heaven, I wouldn't get to find out, because I'd never be good enough to go there.

Words do hurt

I was in the kitchen peeling the spuds for dinner, when I heard an advert on the radio that touched a nerve. It was about a guy who dreamt of becoming a teacher. He was reminiscing about his childhood, and of how he would cry in class because he struggled with his maths work, until his teacher offered him some words of comfort. It had a significant impact on his future life and self, giving him the confidence to pursue his dreams. Her words of support and positivity had stayed with him, helping him through his darkest times.

Now he is winning in life.

Me… well I got called stupid, and that's just what I believed I was. If only I'd have had a teacher like that.

Nervously I held on tight to Mams' hand, as we walked through the deep red painted wooden door. Mam said I had to look my very best, especially on my first day of school. I wore my brand-new navy-blue pinafore dress, with a crisp white blouse, knee length socks, and black patent shiny shoes. My hair was neatly French braided and tied with light blue gingham ribbons. Mam had always dressed us up smart, although I was so petite it was difficult to find clothes that would fit me properly, and with money being tight my Nanna Ava made most of our outfits. Hollie and I would always be in matching dresses and hair bows.

Standing at the entrance in front of a big window, I could see three also very smartly dressed ladies, wearing long skirts and blouses, they sounded very posh as they rushed around behind the glass. I looked down at my black shiny shoes, in the hope that no one would notice me. My Dad would insist that our shoes shone, which he'd learnt from his days in the army. Every Sunday without fail, he'd lay out sheets of newspaper on the countertop, then line up our shoes ready to be polished. He told me that you could tell a lot about someone by how clean their shoes were. Suddenly, my attention guided to a big black box in the corner of the room, at first, I thought it was a coffin, (how I even knew what one looked like I don't know), luckily, I discovered it was nothing but a lost property box. Sighing with relief, I thought maybe it wasn't going to be that bad here after all.

The school was situated in a little village and the classes were very small, with only seven children in the entire year group. Although I was shy, I also wanted to make friends so with there only being a few of us it wasn't as daunting as it could have been. Slowly I came out of my shell and began to make lots of friends. Paige and Sadie were my best friends, and we became inseparable during playtimes. Sadie was a little older than me, she was so sweet, taking me under her wing, she'd teach me how to do gymnastics in the playing field and flip overs on the bars of the swing. I felt so brave when I was with her, she was always there, cheering me on as I practised and practised, beaming proudly to her when I could finally do it perfectly without falling. One day I noticed that Sadie wasn't in the playground at lunchtime.

That one day turned into weeks and Sadie still wasn't back, I felt completely lost without her. Then one morning the whole school gathered for an assembly, we all sat waiting patiently with our legs crossed on the big, patterned rug waiting for the head teacher Ms Owen. I could tell straight away that Ms Owen looked upset, and then she began to cry. It was my friend, Sadie. Ms Owen went on to tell us that Sadie had been very sick with a poorly head, called a brain tumour. My heart hurt that Sadie was so poorly and I couldn't even hug her. She then said that Sadie had gone to heaven. I just didn't understand. I sobbed my little heart out, I know I was young, yet the kindness she'd given me, had left an imprint on my little heart. The school planted a tree in memory of Sadie. It had a gold shiny plaque with her name engraved on it. Whenever I thought of her, I'd go and sit quietly by her tree, and I felt comforted to know that she was safe in heaven. It was hard without Sadie around cheering me on anymore, and I thought about her every day.

It was a hot summers day, and my belly was doing somersaults as it was the dreaded sports day. I hated it, and this story describes the kind of person I was and still am…

So, there I am running along, heart pounding when I suddenly realised that no one was alongside me, approaching the finishing line, parents and teachers were at the finishing line, shouting and encouraging me to win the race. I felt a sense of embarrassment wash over me, so immediately stopped in my tracks. I then burst out crying not wanting to come first, so I let everyone else overtake me to the end. Sports was never going to be a strong subject for me, especially when I found myself volunteering to take part in the longest run ever in high school, (I had no idea how far a mile was).

Looking and feeling like Mr blobby, everyone was laughing as I came last, heading to the finish line, I not only tripped over, but I also did a head over heels, somersault and still didn't cross the friggen finish line.

May Day wasn't any easier, I was always THAT one child to mess up the beautiful plait on the maypole, as the classical music of 'Vivaldi's Four seasons' played on the Ghetto blaster. We'd then have to go backwards until it untangled, with the perfectionists glaring at my blushing face, each time they skipped past me.

My confidence eventually grew when I moved up into the juniors and began to make more friends. I was so happy when the popular girl Francesca invited me to her house for tea. Francesca didn't have any brothers or sisters and lived in a big posh house on a new housing estate. The hallway was as big as my bedroom if not bigger. Everywhere smelt so clean and looked very tidy. Francesca showed me up to her bedroom where we played with the latest barbie dolls, I remember thinking what a beautiful bedroom she had, and how lucky she was. I couldn't believe it when I saw that she even had her very own bathroom! I sat on her bed and couldn't help but notice her pink silk pyjamas neatly folded on her pillow. I'd never seen anything like it, nothing like my pink t-shirt nightie with 'Strawberry Shortcake' on the front of it. Although it was nice to play at Francesca's house, I knew that I'd be expected to return the favour and was worrying about what she'd think of my house already.

The next day at school we were playing together in the playground, suddenly she came up behind me and tied a scarf tightly around my neck. Grasping for breath, I cried for her to stop. Eventually she let go, laughed and ran off. I didn't want to grass on her, because I'd learnt very quickly in the juniors that, "tell-tale tit your tongue will split." Plus, she was popular and clever, so no one would believe me. Rubbing the sore red mark that circled around my neck, I ran and locked myself in a toilet cubicle. Ms peaking, the shouty teacher as I called her, noticed I was missing from class and came to find me. She demanded I came out, slowly I opened the door and did as she asked. To my amazement, she looked horrified at the red mark around my neck. I gave in, and eventually told her what had happened. The next day Francesca wasn't in school. Or the day after. In fact, I never saw her ever again. I wasn't sure what happened to her, all I did know was that it must have been my fault.

I knew it was going to be hard transitioning up to the junior's room. The truth was... I was shit scared of older kids. Especially the ones I called 'yobbos,' who congregated on the market square benches, smoking weed, blissfully unaware that I would be one of them one day. I'd hide in the footwell of the car when Mam nipped in the corner shop, so they wouldn't see me.

From the moment I'd met the junior class teacher Ms Peaking, I knew that I didn't like her, she always seemed cross. I wept on Ms Challenger's, my infant teacher's lap, shaking my head every time she shouted at me to stop being so silly. I was secretly hoping they would send me home, but they didn't. I knew I'd got to be brave, even though Sadie my special friend wasn't there to look out for me anymore, I had to be strong and do it for her.

It wasn't long before I'd settled in and made plenty of friends. I was also very excited as my birthday was coming up, mam and dad had arranged a disco party for me and said I could invite everyone in my class. Excitedly I handed out my hand made party invitations to everyone. On the day of my party, I wore my new black velvet hat and my green jeans with a cream bodysuit, (it was the fashion back then, trust me). We all danced away to '*Mr vain*' and '*No limit*,' in the local parish room village hall. (Which for some reason I'd always called the passion rooms and wondered why everyone thought it was so funny.) As the party ended, Mam cut the cake into small pieces, so everyone could take some home in their party bag. The same sad feeling would suddenly overwhelm me, curling up in the corner somewhere, I'd be bawling my eyes out because it had all come to an end.

As I grew older, I was beginning to find that I was struggling in my lessons, especially maths. Dad had always joked that I was behind the door when the brains were handed out, but he'd also assured me that it was ok to ask for help, and not to be embarrassed if I needed it. One day I sat in class, and I was having difficulty understanding my work.

I eventually plucked up the courage to ask for help and raised my hand. I soon wish I hadn't bothered. *"Please could you say that again,"* I asked politely, feeling rather proud of myself, normally I'd have just sat there bewildered, watching everyone else discuss their answers, while scribbling them down in their books. Today though, I felt brave. Ms Peaking hurried over to me, she repeated herself so quickly that I was even more confused than before. My mind was trying so hard to figure it out, but no matter how hard I tried, I just couldn't get it. I looked up at her again with a blank expression on my blushed face. *"I'm sorry," "I just really don't understand,"* I whispered quietly.

The response the teacher gave me was to affect me throughout my life... *"Jesus Christ child, what are you? bloody stupid or something"*

I sank down in my chair; I wanted the ground to swallow me up. My cheeks burned, I felt everyone staring and whispering. I'd never felt so embarrassed as I did that day. I knew deep down she was right; it didn't stop it hurting though. I was stupid, I was thick, I was a chair short of a table, a sarnie short of a picnic. Why would anyone ever expect any more from me?

From then on, and right up until the end of junior school, I'd sit next to my best friend Paige, and she would let me copy her work. I felt like such a cheat, and I felt so ashamed that I couldn't think for myself like the rest of the class or be as clever as them. Paige never once complained, I think she was as upset as I was about the situation. It wasn't until the SATS exams were brought in for junior schools, that I realised just how much I was behind. Consisting of my worst nightmare,

Maths and English papers. I could predict what the outcome was going to be before even putting pen to paper. Sure enough, it was all just alien to me. I sat quietly and sobbed to myself. I had no choice but to muddle through the rest of my school year as best as I could.

When I started high school, Paige and I were parted, so I didn't know a soul and I was left to go it alone. I'd been assigned into the middle set for my maths lessons, but the teacher took one look at my work and moved me down to another group. I was so embarrassed when I discovered that I was in the lowest maths set there was. The other kids were always taking the piss by calling us, "The cabbage patch group." The teacher Ms Hemsworth was just as bad, she was a tall lady with curly mousy brown hair, she had one eye looking up the street the other coming back down, and they called her one tit wonder. I feel sorry for her now, but I didn't back then, I thought it was hilarious.

Ms Hemsworth never explained anything, and I learnt nothing in her class, in fact I'd say she didn't seem very smart at all to say she was a teacher. "*What's the question?*" she'd ask. Pointing to the question in my maths book I'd show her, she would then snap "*So what's the answer then?*" ... if I fucking knew that I wouldn't be here asking you, I thought to myself.

Nothing would restore my shattered confidence now. My parents had no idea until the school contacted them to explain how far behind, I was. I had no choice but to tell them what had happened, and what Ms Peaking had said to me in primary school. I've often wondered if Ms Peaking felt bad afterwards, or even realised what affect her cruel words had on me. No, I shouldn't think so, why would she care? Unlike bruises that could be hidden under clothes, emotional bullying scars you in ways that are incomprehensible. Things were to get a whole lot worse, when the school bully called me FAT… That was the beginning of my shameful eating disorder.

Of course, I believed her. Naomi was the school bully, you didn't mess with her, who by the way was three times the size of me. She had a tough home life and even though she made me feel like complete shit about myself, I felt both scared and sorry for her. One lunchtime I found her rummaging around in the lunch box area, she was stealing food from the other kids' lunches. I was really confused as to why she was calling me the fat pig, when it was her that was scoffing all that extra grub. It didn't matter now, it was too late, her words had already done the damage she intended, and I stopped eating. I'd hide my untouched sarnies anywhere, pretending to have eaten them, leaving my red Wurzel Gummidge lunch box empty.

The teachers somehow caught on to what I was doing, because the dinner lady started checking the white ice cream tub bin in the middle of the table for my food. After they had informed my Mam, they told me I'd have to sit supervised by a teacher at lunchtimes, and I hated it. I now had to rethink my strategy. It wasn't as hard as I thought it'd be since I kept a blue towel from the toilets in my lap. I'd take tiny bites and then spit into the towel when they weren't watching. Very often there would be some kid acting up, so the teacher would be distracted enough for me to conveniently nip to the toilet to dispose of my lunch. Someone must have grassed me up again because I then found myself in the staff room having to sit with a bunch of teachers, eating their tuna sandwiches and walkers' crisps. (We couldn't afford them, no frills all the way in my house). They would talk about their perfect lives, what they were having for dinner and what their plans were over the weekend. God it was boring, I couldn't wait to get out of there. Usually, they were satisfied after they'd see me eat a few bites, and they couldn't wait to get rid of me so they could continue with their gossiping. It left me free to leave, sneaking out the side gate of the school playground to my new undiscovered hiding place, the builder's skip.

The name Calling didn't just end at fat either, as I mentioned earlier on, I was an early starter in puberty. I didn't have a clue what was happening to my body. I did sometimes wonder, and I still do if my early start to puberty was because of what had happened with Nathan. Or maybe it was my punishment for being bad. I didn't like it either way. All I wanted was to be able to play with my barbie dolls and Sylvanian families, but I couldn't enjoy those things anymore, because it was drummed into me by the teachers that 'I was now a lady.' Ladies didn't play with toys, and ladies weren't expected to join in with immature fun and games. Everything had started to build up inside me and my confidence started to suffer badly. My friends didn't understand why I couldn't go swimming and would question me, accusing me of lying they demanded I drop my knickers to prove it to them. Which of course I did. The boys would cruelly taunt me by rummaging through my backpack in the cloakroom, chucking my fanny pads all over the playground. I tried my best to laugh it off, but it stung inside. I felt nothing but shame and embarrassment for who I was, but then again that was nothing compared to what I was about to experience at high school…

Nothing had prepared me for going from what seemed like a member of a big family, to walking into what I can only describe as a prison. I felt out of my depths noticing how the other children my age behaved and the first week was so bad I spent most of it either getting lost or stared at by the other kids. This then resulted in me having a major meltdown at home, blaming my Mam and Dad for sending me to a small school, and making me stand out as being different. I was scared because of how innocent and vulnerable I was, I knew I'd be a target for bullies, so I kept my head down and tried my best to fit in and make friends. Eventually I did settle and thankfully made lots of new friends. I became a proper agony aunt, never judging but listening and being a shoulder to cry on. I could finally be myself, which was to love, care and be there for everyone. Helping others was what made me happy. When we weren't together in school, we would be at each other's houses listening to the 'Spice girls' wannabe,' and 'Peter Andre's Mysterious girl.' We'd spend hours on the phone chatting and laughing, although this wasn't the latest mobile phone, (as I'm a complete dinosaur and we didn't have them back then). It wasn't even a cordless phone, so much to everyone's annoyance in the house, I would happily lay sprawled across the floor, so they would have to step over me. I was forever being trod on and kicked if anyone walked past, not that it bothered me, I was quite content laying on the floor, deep in convo with my friends discussing the drama of Holly oaks.

Finally, I'd found happiness, and lots of lovely friends. I'd a good feeling about my future and hoped that the past was now a distant memory.

Déjà vu

As the bell rang, lunch break was over. All the corridors were manic with everyone making their way to afternoon lessons.

My class lined up outside the IT room waiting for the teacher Mr.

James, eventually he arrived stinking of fags and coffee.

Mr. James then introduced the class to a student teacher on work experience called Simon. He was about twenty years old and tall with dark hair. I remember feeling quite sorry for him because of his acne, but at the same time he had an unnerving presence about him. It soon became clear to me that my instincts were proven to be true about him.

I was trying to follow the instructions from the worksheet in front of me, when the computer mouse stopped working. I raised my hand for help, hoping Mr. James would notice. He was over the other side of the classroom helping someone else, so I quickly put my hand back down. I felt wary of Simon the student teacher, I couldn't put my finger on what it was about him, I just knew that he made me feel uneasy. The next thing I knew Simon had appeared behind me.

Creepily, he stood staring at me, so I asked him if he knew why the mouse wasn't working. He then stood behind me and leaned over as he reached for the computer mouse. As he leant over, he brushed past my boobs. Naively, I dismissed it as an accident. As Simon walked away, I realised that I still had the same problem, raising my hand for the second time,

I said, *"Excuse me sir, it's still not working."* Over he sauntered, leaning over me once again, only this time I could smell his breath on me. Sliding his hand up my jumper and under my shirt, he groped me. I sat at my desk staring at the blank computer screen in shock. I couldn't believe what he had just blatantly done, and in the middle of a classroom. Why would he even do that? I then thought back to when I had raised my hand before, back in junior school. Hadn't I learnt anything? What was wrong with me? I thought the lesson was never going to end, all I wanted to do was get out of that stuffy classroom. I struggled through the rest of the lesson close to tears. That familiar feeling had returned in the pit of my stomach.

Finally, the bell rang. My heart raced as I ran to the toilet. I locked myself in the cubical, collapsed onto the toilet seat with my head in my hands, and broke down. Why was this happening to me? Why did they choose me? What did I do wrong? I was still a child, finding my feet in high school, I should have felt safe.

Understandably, I didn't want to go to school the next morning, but I reluctantly dragged myself out of bed, threw on my uniform and waited for my friend Jolie to knock for me. Jolie was another one of my good pals, we told each other everything. I'd debated whether I should confide in her, but I also didn't want to burden her with my problems. I was just going to have to put a brave face on. We'd meet outside the canteen at breaktime, and have a chin wag over a kit kat, but before we knew it it'd be time to navigate our way to our next lessons, in this Crystal Maze of a High School.

Approaching the school gates, my belly was doing somersaults. I really didn't want to be there, and I couldn't stop thinking about what had happened the day before. What if I was to see Simon? I must have been noticeably quiet, because Jolie kept looking over at me asking if I was ok. I just nodded and looked away, the last thing I wanted was to draw attention to myself. The more she persisted, the more I found it difficult to hide, so I decided to tell her the truth. I knew I could trust Jolie, and to my shock not only did she believe me, but she also told me that he had tried to do it to her. Thankfully, Jolie managed to push him away, and he had left her alone. I felt sick.

Jolie encouraged me to tell someone before he did it to anyone else. I was so nervous about it; however, my gut instinct was telling me it was the right thing to do. I asked my form tutor Mr Jackson if I could talk to him. It was an uncomfortable conversation to have, but to be fair he listened intently to everything I had to say. Mr Jackson reassured me that he would be reporting it to the head of year Ms Johnson. That afternoon both me and Jolie were asked to go to Ms Johnson's office. We waited nervously after knocking her office door. The only time anyone would ever be in that part of the school building, was if they were in trouble. Ms Johnson opened the door and calmy asked us to go in and sit down. She told us that they were taking the matter extremely seriously, and that Jolie and I would have to be interviewed separately. Ms Johnson reassured us that she would do all she could to support us. Later that day I had to repeat what had happened to Mr. Jacobs, the head teacher.

I then had to be questioned again by another member of staff. It was so frustrating to have to keep going over and over what had happened. It was like they didn't believe me. I knew they had to make sure I wasn't lying, what I could not understand was why on earth would anyone lie about something like this? When I arrived home after school, Mam told me that the Police were coming over to talk to me about what had happened. I started freaking out, *"No, no, I'll be in trouble. What if he comes to find me?"* I can't talk to them; they won't believe me.

Shaking my leg frantically, I waited for the knock at the door. Eventually two officers appeared in the living room and began to bombard me with a load of uncomfortable questions, scribbling notes from the answers I gave. They explained that I'd be expected to give a statement and if Simon pleaded not guilty, I'd have to stand up in court to give evidence against him. Wait, what? Court? No one had mentioned that part to me. Everyone would find out what had happened? Even worse, the officer told me to prepare myself for court as he explained that it was the defence barristers' job to challenge what I was telling them. Naively, I asked them what they meant by this, he said, *"for instance, you'll be asked to describe exactly what happened in detail. They'll also want to know what you were wearing and things like that. Their job is to defend the accused, so it won't be very nice."* (Practically making me feel like this was my fault and not his then). What the fuck? Was he kidding me? Was I actually hearing this right?

I was wearing a thick white school shirt firmly buttoned up to my neck, a tie, a bright red oversized jumper with a school logo on and smart black trousers. I got the gist of what they were saying. After the police had spoken to us, we decided that I'd been through enough already, without having to stand up in court. I felt relieved but at the same time hoped that I had done enough for him to be punished for his actions.

I tried to knuckle down with my schoolwork, putting it to the back of my mind with the rest of the crap I'd collected. From then on, I'd make sure I had someone with me at school, because I was terrified that Simon would be lurking about somewhere. After a month or so, I was summoned to Mr. Jacob's office. He told me that he'd received an update on the case against Simon. After further investigation, it had been discovered that there were further accusations, he obviously couldn't give me any more information, which I completely understood. I was just relieved they were doing something about it. Mr Jacobs then stood up, shook my hand, and showed me out of his office.

The incident was never to be spoken of again. I didn't even know what happened to Simon, until a couple of years later…

I was fifteen, in my final year of school and was just leaving the library after a revision class. There he stood, clear as day staring right at me. I tried to convince myself that it was my imagination, but I couldn't forget that fucking smirk. I held to the wall to steady myself as he blatantly walked straight past me, so close that I shivered.

It disgusted me that he was allowed back into a school environment. How could that even happen? How are victims ever meant to speak out if this is how they are treated?

By the time I reached year eight at high school, things started to go tits up. I thought it was funny and cool to act up both in and out of class. I started drinking and smoking in the rec with my pals, I was up for doing anything to be popular. One break time, I was hanging out with a group of pals, when I suddenly felt the urge to run over to the counter and grab a purple bag of *Monster Munch*. With my adrenaline running high, I legged it out of the dinner hall as fast as I could into the corridor, with the girls behind me laughing our heads off. I'd found my defiant side again, and I was in control. Out of breath, and still giggling to myself, I headed towards my form room when my friend Sammy tapped my shoulder and me, *"Why did you just do that? You do know that you don't have to do shit like that to be liked don't you?",* *Your pals like you for who you are and if they don't* *then fuck them".* I didn't even know what to say, because I knew deep down that she was right. Even though I chose not to follow that advice until much later in life, her words never left me.

The boys started to mock me with the whole, *"Big tits,"* and *"Get them out for the lad's,"* crap. It didn't even bother me anymore, not that it helped that I was a petite four foot eleven, weighing just four and a half stone, and my boobs appeared before anything else did. I may well have been behind the door when the brains were handed out, but I sure was at the front of the que when the tits were. My self-worth was non-existent, and I knew that I had to do whatever I could to get by.

Disguising the hell

"Oi…oi," I turned around to see a lady in a white car waving her hands at me. I waved politely with a blank expression, (you know that kind of wave you do, when you have absolutely no idea who they are). I continued with my walk up to school when I noticed the same car stopped at the crossing, she wound her window down and I heard the words in slow motion, *"Excuse me love; your skirts tucked in your knickers."* For fuck's sake! only me.

I wasn't the slightest bit interested in school, and I certainly wasn't bothered about a career, or a successful future. There was only one thing on my mind, and that was messing about and having a laugh. I only cared about the here, and the now. However, there was something I had always wanted to become, and that was a 'Mam,' one day. The teachers were never impressed with my answer when filling out our career plans in class, so I just stuck with the very original, 'Hairdresser.'

My dad would repeatedly tell me, "*You need to start concentrating on the inside of the circle and not the outside.*" I admit I can understand his frustration now, all he ever wanted was the best education and future for me. Oh, dad if I knew then what I know now. We live and learn I guess, don't we? Every time we would pass a BMW in the car, I would smile and say to my dad, "*Dad I want one of those one day.*" His answer was always the same, "*well love, you have two choices, you either get your head down at school, or you marry a rich man.*" ... I still don't have a BMW.

Often, we were put on the spot in maths, the teacher took immense joy in picking on me as she asked me to explain to the class the answer to her question. *"Give me two ways of saying half."* Confidently I knew I had the right answer as I blurted out, *"HALF and HAAAARF."* Staring at me for a moment, she then shook her head and corrected me, that the answer was in fact 50% and O.5. As if that wasn't bad enough, the next question of, *"What does the temperature read on the card I'm holding?"* Thank God this was easier, *"It says twenty-five degrees."* Shouting so loud, I nearly crapped myself she yelled back to me, *"Twenty-five degrees what?"* Under pressure I said the first thing that came into my head and shouted back, *"Miss".* *"NO! for goodness's sake… Celsius"* she tutted. I could sense she was frustrated with me by her tone, not that I understood why. Anyhow moving on, I don't want to bore you anymore with my embarrassing stories. I feel it's important to add the difficulties I faced at school and in life in general, believe me there's plenty more where that came from.

Adamant I was thick and always would be, I did try my best with whatever challenge I would find myself faced with, even when I felt my best wasn't good enough, I just sailed along in life in my own way. As I matured, I felt a strong surge of power and belief that it was my life and I wanted to live it with as much freedom and fun as I was able to. Even if it meant getting into trouble. My pals would knock for me after school and weekends, we would hang out at the local park and smoke and drink, and once a month the local leisure centre held a disco where we danced away to

'Gangster's Paradise,' 'Grease' and 'Doctor Jones.' Life was all about boys, boys and more boys, my school workbooks were covered in I LOVE (whoever it was that day) IDDST (If destroyed definitely still true) and many other rude words that I was constantly getting in trouble for. The teachers would demand I covered up my graffitied books with wrapping paper, but I just used to rip the posters of the 'Backstreet boys' or 'East17' out my 'Smash hits' mags. My workbooks summed up my thoughts and interests on school and learning in general. It wasn't all bad I guess because I also found my passion for creative lessons such as, art and dance. I loved drawing, painting, and any kind of artwork, even if the lads on the table teased me by nicknaming me 'Alice' from the vicar of Diblcy or carried on in my ear about the time that I was adamant that I could find Australia on the map of Europe.

I joined dance clubs, in and out of school and was so proud of myself when I performed at a theatre. I also discovered my love of English language and literature, (well that's when I wasn't passing notes to my friends about who fancied who and who was out later.) until it went horribly wrong, and my note fell into the teacher's hand. She didn't only give me an afterschool detto, she also found it hilarious to read it out in front of everyone. Awks! Great, another hour and a half of repeatedly having to write the sentence of, '*I must behave in class. I must not write notes in class.*' My hand ached after writing around four sheets of A4 lined paper as neatly as I could, to avoid any further punishment. Not that it stopped me being cheeky, once I got the giggles I just couldn't stop, especially when the teacher was talking about doorknobs. Much to my embarrassment, Ms Calcott demanded I stood up in front of the whole class and explain why the word knob was so funny. In all seriousness, I was just using my behaviour as a way of taking control of my life, while rebelling against the rules as I felt that I could.

I shared my first kiss, hiding in the school yard with a popular boy in my year. His red cheeks were so cold, and I choked on the smell of his lynx Africa. After that, I was never to be without a boy. I didn't care if they were older than me, younger than me or the same age, all I wanted was to feel loved. Unfortunately, after many boyfriends I was to realise that it wasn't ever about love. Not for them anyway. It's almost always about sex. Then again, I should have known that already.

Even though I had no confidence in myself, I would dye my hair mahogany red, stick on my *Rimmel 'Heather shimmer,'* lippy and wear skirts up to my arse (sorry Nanna). I would strut my stuff in my four and a half inch heels, which let me tell you took a lot of practise to walk in. I would fall in love so easily, with anyone who showed me the slightest bit of attention. They made me feel special, until I did what they wanted that was. Generally, I was attracted to the bad boys, the ones you would see in the school corridors that had been sent out of class, with their shirts untucked acting like the big man. The boys just thought I was easy, probably because I was one of the first ones to drop my knickers or give them a hand job, in fear of rejection.

As I reached my teens, my health started deteriorating with my periods getting worse, and my emotions were spiralling out of control. I'd cry so much all the time. Eventually the doctor suggested that I start the contraceptive pill, reluctantly mam agreed because she could see the pain, I was in.

I was fifteen years old when I lost my virginity to my boyfriend, we had been seeing each other on and off for a while. He was a good-looking lad, and all the girls fancied him. I felt so lucky that it was me that got to hold his hand around school. Things were getting a bit frisky in his bedroom one afternoon when I suddenly felt shit scared. What if I was rubbish at it? I'd be the joke of the school AGAIN. He reassured me it was ok, and I didn't want to lose him, so with the *beautiful south* playing *perfect 10* in the background it happened. I didn't really know what to expect but I thought it was special, because I believed that we were in love. He was my first love, and my heart was completely shattered when we broke up.

When I was in my last year of school Sammy my best friend asked me if I wanted to go on holiday with her to Ibiza, I jumped at the chance. I had never been on an airplane before, so I was crapping my pants. Dad always gave me his Saint Christopher necklace whenever I was away from home to keep me safe. (He'd call him 'little man') So I knew that if I held on tight to him, I'd be ok.

The holiday was just fab, and full of complete madness and let's just say what we got up to in Ibiza sure as hell stayed in Ibiza. We'd sunbathe on the beach or by the pool all day, have dinner at a nice restaurant then head to clubs, get smashed and dance to the club versions of *"Two times"* and *"I don't want to miss a thing,"* until our feet ached. For the first time in my life, I felt free from psychological pain, I was living life and it felt amazing.

I walked the humid streets of Ibiza in my white high heeled sandals, my leopard print shirt and black leather skirt. Blokes groping us shouting *"Sucky sucky five dollar."*

I made a group of friends there, and I'd fallen in love, (again) with a lad who was quite a bit older than I was, he was so sweet, and we spent every part of the holiday together, sunbathing all day and clubbing all night. I felt so sad, and we both cried when we had to leave but we continued to write to each other for a year or so and planned to meet up back home, but it never happened.

I didn't just go home with a glowing tan; I was also full of a newfound confidence and sense of freedom. I felt I could do whatever I wanted to…

Reality soon hit as I returned home, after having the craziest holiday ever. I decided I was going to test the waters and began to rebel against my parents at every chance I had.

Although I may have appeared to be confident on the outside, I was dying on the inside. The issues I had with my body were beginning to affect me again, now more than they ever had before. Believing that I was fat (looking back at my dainty figure why oh why did I believe that about myself). I would take £1 to school for my lunch, which would be a vending machine lunch consisting of a packet of crisps, a bar of white crunch chocolate bar, and a packet of fruit polos. I was too busy with my pals, and it was too much of a ball ache to go to the canteen for a meal, even when it smelt lush. I rarely ate anything at home either, I would spend mealtimes playing with my food, shifting it around the plate until it was so cold that if I did try to eat, I would gag. Obsessed with wanting to stay thin, I'd make myself sick after everything that passed my lips. I couldn't bear the pain I felt from reaching, but I was prepared to do whatever it took to keep the weight off, it didn't matter how dangerous it was. If I weren't making myself sick, I would be starving myself. Later discovering that laxatives were a much easier and accessible option as the swallowing of the pill was the only real work I had to do. It was soon a part of my daily ritual of taking my contraceptive pill alongside the laxatives, it was an addictive and unhealthy habit to keep up, and it drained the hell out of me. I did stop taking them for a short while after they had made me really sick, so much so that it felt like my stomach was being ripped out. Sweat was dripping from my forehead, while I sat on the toilet in absolute agony. It wasn't only a physical pain; it was also a deep emotional pain I felt. I was damaging my body by self-harming daily, and what's worse is I didn't even care.

My periods became so unbearable that I'd literally scream, cry, bite myself through the pain. I would roll around the living room floor in agony, it got so normal that everyone would just step over me. My education began to suffer due to hospital appointments, scans, and x-rays. The consultant explained that it was likely I was going to suffer a lot more than others due to my age, and it was likely I would have issues with future childbirth because I had a very narrow pelvis.

He tried me on various medications, but nothing helped and eventually recommended a different contraceptive pill, which made the pain slightly more bearable and told me that I'd just have to learn to cope.

I felt so trapped in life again as I walked through a never-ending storm.

A little bit broken

The dark cloud above me decided that it was not going to piss off, instead it was going to linger on and follow me everywhere I went. It didn't matter how much I tried to ignore it I couldn't shift the feelings of sadness and emptiness it brought with it, finding it impossible to find any positives in my life and every day just became an effort that I couldn't be arsed with. I'd wrap myself up tight in my warm duvet nd began to withdraw from my family and friends, hiding behind a non-existent list excuse to stay in my bedroom and cry for hours.

I was experiencing the worst widespread pain in my body I'd ever felt. I put it down to the tension I felt from my emotions. It started at my feet and made its way up to my head, leaving me with migraines that even a dark, quiet room couldn't shift. There wasn't a day that went by that I didn't open my eyes and feel like I'd been run over by a truck.

I saw the doc who just told me that I was too young to suffer with any type of chronic pain, and that the only explanation was that it must have been growing pains. Bullshit I thought, that was just a cop out, the pain I was experiencing was most definitely real, it wasn't imaginary, and it wasn't growing pains, so I started popping pain killers daily, which made absolutely no difference whatsoever.

Ms Johnson, the head of my school year, rang my Mam because she was concerned about my lack of attendance, and she suggested that I started having therapy sessions with the school councillor.

Ms Johnson then spoke to me on the phone and told me that although the school councillor couldn't help with the physical pain, she may be able to help me find ways of coping with my emotions. Reluctantly I agreed. I didn't want to stand out as being different to everyone else, but I also knew that it had got to the point that I needed to accept help. I think all I really needed was for someone to reassure me that everything was going to be ok.

The following week, at break time while everyone else headed towards the main hall for their lunch, I crept off in the opposite direction to Ms Baker, the school councillor's office.

Ms Baker was standing at her office door ready to welcome me. She was a middle-aged lady with short light brown hair in a bob.

The first thing I remember about Ms Baker, was how at ease she made me feel with her calm presence, and over time I was able to put my trust in her. Nothing was ever too much trouble for her, and she'd sit quietly and listen while I rambled on about how I felt.

I know now that I'd have been lost without those sessions, and luckily, I was able to continue with them until my final year of school. I don't think Ms Baker will ever realise just what an impact she had on my life through her kindness and support. Although Ms Baker felt that the sessions were proving to be beneficial to me, she also felt that I needed additional support and suggested that my parents sought help in my GP, regarding both my mental and physical health.

It'd upset me how my dad would get frustrated at me by asking me all the time, *"You shouldn't feel like this, what have you got to worry about? you've got no responsibilities."* He was right, I didn't. But I still couldn't give him any answers as to why I felt like I did. All I knew was that I didn't feel well.

The following week, I had an appointment with the doc. Ms Baker had suggested I write down anything that I thought the doctor should know and take it with me to the appointment. She explained that it could be difficult when under pressure to put feelings and emotions into words. The night before my appointment I sat at the kitchen table and thought hard about what I wanted to say. I tried to be as honest as I could be, so I began with my feelings and thoughts.

I put pen to paper, and I wrote.

Sad   Unhappy   Useless   Frustrated   Worthless   Pathetic

Stupid

Fat   Ugly   Exhausted   Stressed   In pain   crying all the time.

I knocked on the door and a male voice abruptly shouted, *"Come in."*

Mam briefly explained the reason for our visit. Then nodded at me to hand over my now scrunched up note. *"Erm…I've wrote my feelings down for you to read,"* I said with my head down.

The doc took the piece of paper from me. I nervously waited for his response, watching his squinted eyes scan my scribbled words.

I heard his words in slow motion as they left his mouth mocking me when he did finally speak, "*Oh, I shouldn't worry it's just your personality.*" He said laughing as he threw the note across his desk, returning it to my clammy hand. I could feel tears welling up in my eyes. I had to get out of that room. I felt even more pathetic than before I walked in. It was at that moment that I lost all faith in doctors or any health professional for that matter. It was quite clear to me that I had to accept there was absolutely nothing wrong with me and I just had to deal with it.

Mam encouraged me to try to talk to the pastor of our church who was a lovely man and tried to help me, but I just felt so awkward and uncomfortable around men. I felt guilty that he'd given up his precious time for me and through no fault of his own he'd never be able to fully understand how I felt. The truth was it didn't matter who I spoke to, nothing was going to ease that pain, because I still hadn't found the strength to be able to confide in anyone, about *'The secret.'*

Still, it was there, weighing me down, and it was to continue to plague me for more years to come.

I was feeling even more anxious because the dreaded GCSEs had sneaked up on me. I started suffering with panic attacks because of how worked up I was about sitting them, and I knew how far behind I was.

The sports hall was lined up with chairs and single desks, the only sound to be heard when entering was the squeaking of shoes on the floor.

I sat with my pen going through the questions answering them as best as I could. The rest of the time I spent chewing on my gum, whilst staring into space. The boys would be pissing around with their calculators, spelling out rude words to show each other until they got caught.

I just about scraped through each exam paper, (even though I was unable to identify the difference between a stethoscope and a telescope).

I just couldn't wait for them all to be over, so I could get the hell out of there.

I already knew how little faith my maths teacher had in me, when he had estimated me a grade U I was gutted. You can only imagine my excitement when results day arrived, and I found out I had been graded a G. *EEEEEK!*...

I headed straight over to Mr. Coles, my maths teacher. There he stood in the main hall proudly surrounded with his beaming A* students, not giving me the time of day. Epic fail. AGAIN!

I did achieve B grades in both Art and English, which I was very proud of, but having not done anywhere near as well as my friends, I won't ever forget how heavy hearted I felt when I listened to all their exciting plans for their future. When they asked me what mine were, I just went blank. I had no idea what my future held at all. But hey the good news was...

NO SCHOOL!!

It was Summer of the year 2000. I was literally done so I decided for once, to not follow the crowd, but do something completely the opposite and take a year out of education and go to work.

I wasn't sad that I was leaving, but I was sorry to say goodbye to my friends, because I knew that our lives were about to lead down different paths.

So…with everyone's signatures on my shirt, and my tie wrapped round my head in a bow, I walked out those prison gates for the very last time, clutching my little memory book full of messages from all my friends and teachers wishing me well. I still look at that little book sometimes and read all the lovely messages. It's taken almost twenty years to understand what one teacher had meant though as he had scribbled, *"Make your own luck."* I so understand what he meant now. It's funny how we don't understand things until years later, and then after a little life experience it just clicks.

After I'd left school, I decided it was time for a complete change, starting with my hair. I got the bus into town and went to *Boots,* searching the hair colour section and I picked up a bleach blonde colour. Leaving the shop, I felt butterflies in my belly, this was going to be a new me. I didn't want to be recognised, as far as I was concerned that girl didn't exist anymore.

About a week after I had finished school, I came across an advert for a shop assistant in the local chippy. Why not? I thought, after all I had to start somewhere. Having not experienced an interview before, I had no idea what to wear, so I just put-on white blouse and black trousers. I couldn't believe it when they offered me the job the same day. Proudly I rang my mum and dad to tell them the good news, although they weren't exactly ecstatic about it, but they agreed that it was a start. However, it didn't last, because after a week of stinking of sweat, the lingering taste of chip fat, and being constantly perved on by the letch of a boss, I decided I'd had enough. The next morning when the shop was closed, I pushed my apron through the letter box in a carrier bag along with my written notice.

During the summer, I found myself once again head over heels in love. Ben had blonde hair, blue eyes, and a sexy deep voice. He was already working at hotel and went to college, so we had to fit in meeting up whenever we could. Ben encouraged me to apply for a job that came up at the hotel where he worked. I didn't know what chamber maid was, but he said it was just another name for a cleaner. Eventually he won me over by promising me that we'd be able to spend more time together.

It was a beautiful old hotel, called 'The Swan,' It was on a main street, so to access it you had to walk through an arch, which led to the back of the hotel were the laundry rooms were.

The hotel manager was a pleasant lady Pam, she fetched me a glass of water and asked me a variety questions in my interview. She told me that if I were successful, the job would be on a one-week trial basis. After thanking me for attending she said, *"If it suits you, could you start next week?"* Excitedly which I replied, *"Yes, thankyou that would be lovely,"* before she changed her mind. Someone actually wanted me, and it felt so good. Pam then introduced me to the other girls in the laundry room. They all seemed friendly, and I couldn't wait to start my new job.

I loved cleaning when I was at home, in fact my nick name was 'cinders.' I was forever tidying up Hollie's side of the bedroom, it would drive me mad if things weren't tidy or out of place. I'd hoover, dust, polish, and mop, not because I was made to, but because I wanted to.

To make a good impression, I arrived fifteen minutes early on my first day. Pam showed me to where the uniforms were kept, she then measured me and then went in search for a size 6-8 dress. The only size she could find was a 14-16, "*I know it's a bit big, but you'll have to make do until I can order your size in*". (Never mind a size 68, I'd take a size 14 now any day of the week). I felt so embarrassed as I emerged out of the changing room looking like a sack of spuds. Those uniforms were not made for little people and while everyone else's uniform finished at their knees, mine carried on past my ankles. Pam then shown me to my first room and said that someone would be along to train me up. I was waiting outside the room when I saw Ben, *"Just checking in that you're ok,"* he said, clearly trying not to laugh. *"Don't you start"* I said. *"I look a twat, I know."* A lady then turned up all flustered apologising for how late she was, *'I'm Shirley the supervisor, I'm going to show you the ropes and then I'll leave you to it, don't worry though I'll keep popping up and down to check you're ok though, alright?"*

Shirley gave me my own area in the hotel that I was responsible for every day.

They had a strict policy on cleanliness which the manager would randomly spot check, keeping you on your toes. It was a popular hotel, so the rooms were always full of guests on business or breaks away. It wasn't long before I realised that even though I'd learnt sod all in school, I was now learning life skills every day and even maths. I would have to count how many sheets, pillowcases, towels, and toiletries I needed and times it by how many rooms I had that day. It was just simple little things that I hadn't thought about before.

The only time I didn't look forward to work, was if I had to cover for someone in charge of the older part of the hotel. Mainly because I swear it was haunted, and I was shit scared of being on my own. The corridors were long and dark. The bumpy floorboards would creak as I dragged my henry hoover along them. The smell of food from the kitchen drifted up from below, although all I ever thought I could smell was baked beans. At the end of the corridor was the bridal suite, the creepiest room in the hotel. The room always felt cold and dark, not that the dark wooden furniture helped. In the middle of the room was a queen size four poster bed, which let me tell you was a bugger to make up. Propping the door open with my basket of cleaning supplies, I'd clean the room as fast as I could as I sang to myself, *"pink in the sink and blue in the loo,"* wondering why anyone would choose that room for their wedding night, but hey ho each to their own.

Early one wintry morning, I stood minding my own business while chattering my teeth, as I waited for the six am bus when a lady appeared from nowhere and started chatting to me. She was really sweet with her nervous little laugh bless her, she took my hand, she introduced herself, *"I'm Kath."* She told me that she worked at the supermarket around the corner from the hotel I worked at, and kindly offered to give me a lift every day. I was amazed that she still worked as she must have been early seventies, but good for her, I thought to myself. I was a little wary catching a lift with someone I'd only just met, but my instincts told me that I'd be just fine, and they hadn't let me down before. Kath genuinely was the loveliest soul you could ever meet, and we became good friends. She had a little white dog named Tiegan, that she would drop off at her friend's house every morning on the way to work. She would sit on my knee and malt all over my black trousers, whilst licking my face off, (that is the dog not the lady), she was just the cutest.

I don't think anyone had expected me to stick at my job, but I was determined to prove them wrong. Maybe my Mum and Dad were just playing a little reverse psychology with me, who knows either way I stubbornly did stick at it for an entire year. I loved the people I worked with, we had such a laugh in and out of work. It was one of the first times that I had felt respected and grown up at the same time as learning how to be independent. My wages were £60 a week, this would then be divided into, £30 a week board, £15 bus fare home from work every day, £10 for phone credit and £5 for any toiletries or basics I needed. It taught me the importance of money and how to look after it. My priority was always board money first, which I can honestly say I never missed one payment.

At Christmas, the big boss treated all the staff to a Christmas party and a three-course meal at a posh restaurant. The menus were handed out a month in advance, so there I am staring at this fancy menu trying to work out what each dish actually consisted of, considering the only grub I knew of was, corned beef hash, roastie, cauli cheese or curry. Oh, and of course spag bol. I then spotted the word 'salmon,' thinking that'd be a safe bet, so I ticked the box. Huge mistake, it was gross. Luckily, I was a pro at hiding my food, so I pretended to enjoy it, whilst hiding the remainder of the meal under a maroon-coloured napkin, dreading the thought of how much it must have cost.

There were endless amounts of bottles of red wine on the table, and every time I was distracted talking my glass was full again.

I knew someone must have been filling it up, not that I cared as I just went with the flow. I remember finding everything so funny, anyone that knows me, knows that once I get the giggles I can't stop. I was having the time of my life, well that was until nature called and I stood up to go to the loo…Oh, my days! my legs felt like jelly, and I fell flat on my face, I was so embarrassed as I tried to scramble my way back up to my feet.

I made it to the toilet just in time to fall over yet again and spew up the wall, the sink and finally the in bog. I sat on the floor crying as I looked down at my new white top, which was now stained a black currant red. Shirley came and sat with me, gave me a glass of water, and helped me up. *"Let's get you out of this."* She said pulling my top up over my head. Shirley then covered me up in my long beige jacket, wrapping its belt around me. I was dreading going back into the room, but I managed to stumble my way to the table, feeling everyone's eyes on me.

Ben sat with me on the coach home, reminding me to put my boobs away every five minutes. The coach pulled over at the stop in my village as Ben prompted me that I had to get off.

I remember feeling so free as I walked down the road, breathing in the chilly winter air, I didn't give a shit about anything or anyone, I felt free as a bird. I wasn't fazed by the fact that I was walking in the middle of the road, barefooted on a freezing cold December night and God only knew where I'd ditched my heels.

I crept in the front door and eventually made it to bed, fully clothed, and crashed out. The next morning, I felt like I had been hit by a bus. I felt so ashamed about what had happened, vowing I'd never touch red wine ever again. (Hmmm yeah, about that…).

On my way to work the following week, I went to the shop and bought the biggest box of chocolates I could find to give to Shirley. She gave me a big hug, reassuring me that everyone's done it and not to worry, eventually it was old news.

On my seventeenth birthday Ben gave me a beautiful necklace, it was a two-piece heart, one side said, 'always,' and the other said, 'forever.' I couldn't have felt happier, but it wasn't meant to be because a few weeks later we'd broke up. We agreed to stay friends as we worked together, but it wasn't easy because I couldn't just switch my feelings off as easily as he'd seemed to. I was left heartbroken yet again and the cloud was back, and I started to smoke and drink as a way of coping.

Deep down I felt like there was something wrong with me like I was broken and unlovable. I was fed up with giving away all my energy and love so freely to others when I was left feeling exhausted, used and heartbroken. My kindness was always being mistaken for weakness, and then used against me, I didn't think that my feelings mattered, just everyone else's did.

I couldn't avoid seeing Ben, as we still worked together. He kept going on and on about a mate of his at college and hinted that I should meet up with him. He said that he'd be good for me, as he was a nice lad and a good laugh, but I just thought it was his way of shifting his guilt, so he could move on.

Eventually I thought what the hell and gave in and agreed for him to pass my number on.

I didn't hold up much hope though.

Love finds you

April 15th, 2001, my phone beeped.

My heart thudded as I excitedly opened the text message.

I was glad in some ways that we didn't know each other's past because I'm sure if he knew my background, he wouldn't be texting me right now. *'Hi, its Brad how are you.'* Shit…what do I say? *'Hiya I'm ok thanks, you?'* He replied with, *'I'm good thanks, just on the way home from a Papa Roach concert.'* And that's how it all began…

We continued to exchange messages for a couple of hours until I couldn't keep my eyes open any longer, we finally said goodnight until tomorrow. We messaged every day for two weeks and would have random convos at all hours on the phone and the following week we arranged to meet up. I had no idea what this boy looked like or anything…We must have been mad.

It was a Saturday morning, and I was a complete bag of nerves. I got up, showered, and did my hair and make-up. I put on my denim jacket, lit a fag and I left the house smelling of Charlie red. I was crapping myself, I looked at my watch and I was running five minutes late. Great start, NOT!

We'd arranged to meet at a bench near the church about ten minutes away from my house. As I walked along the road, I could see him sitting at the bench, as I got closer, I stubbed out my smoke and walked up to him. *"Hiya, your'ite."* I could hear the high-pitched giddiness in my voice as the words left my mouth. *"Sorry I'm late."* I apologised with absolutely no excuse whatsoever. Well other than the fact I needed about three nervous shits; second thoughts no don't say anything. That's right, mouth firmly zipped shut, in fear of saying something that I will regret almost instantly. I tried not to obviously gawp at him, but I couldn't help it as he was the complete opposite to anyone I'd been out with before, not that it mattered, it was hopefully a good sign. *"Do you fancy walking up to mine? It's about twenty-five minutes away up the hill."* He asked me. *"Yeah, course."* I answered not realising how steep the hill actually was, I was soo unfit.

I didn't feel awkward with Brad at all and the more we talked the more comfortable I felt. It was like we'd known each other for ages as we talked about all kinds of stuff. He told me all about his sports he played, cricket, football, and boxing. I just smiled and nodded my head having absolutely no idea what a 'run' or 'wicket' was. But I did play for the girl's football team at high school, so I knew a little bit about that.

By the time we reached the top of the hill I felt like I had known him years, and he probably thought the same, (as well as thinking to himself oh my days she is a nut case, what am I thinking…)

Brad's family were out for the day, so his house was very quiet. The ice was soon broken when he let his three dogs in though. He had a lovely home and his family fostered children so I imagined it wouldn't normally be as quiet as it was that day. We spent a few hours together talking and watching telly, he was studying sports at college and had started a part time job at a pub to fund his driving lessons. I loved how confident and independent he was.

I couldn't believe how quick the time had gone and I felt quite sad when it got dark, and it was time leave. Brad was sweet and offered to walk me home before it got dark. I couldn't believe I'd spent the entire day with someone I'd never met before, and not once did I feel uncomfortable. He walked me all the way to the corner of my road bless him and as I wasn't quite sure what 'we' were, I gave him a quick peck on the cheek, *"Take care, text me when you get home, so I know you safe."* I wasn't sure if that was the right thing to say but it was too late to think about it now.

After that we were inseparable, his family became mine and vice versa. We both shared a love of music and movies so would spend hours listening to tunes or watching films together. I would reel off the entire script of *Forrest Gump*, or we would watch my fave ever collection of *Rocky* videos, which he couldn't believe I owned.

I had completely fallen in love with this boy. The sad thing was I was still at war with how I felt about myself and I found it hard to let him love me. Unintentionally I'd push him away if he tried to get close to me, even though craved for it. How could anyone love someone like me, I felt fat, ugly and least of all worthy of anyone's love. What hurt and confused me the most was that I had so much love to give, yet I struggled to show any kind of affection. Instead, I would surround myself with an imaginary wall, in fear of rejection that I had had my fair share of. When I think about it now, it sounds so trivial compared to what others are going through in life, and I feel guilty for feeling the way I did. But when I was in that state of mind, I couldn't shake it off especially the paranoia and rejection. If I knew back then that I had Bipolar, things may have been different, but I didn't and they weren't, so I just had to ride with it.

I tried to show my love for Brad in the only way I knew, and that was to shower him with gifts and cards expressing how I felt through words rather than actions.

We hadn't been together long when our relationship was first tested when I went on holiday to Tenerife with my pal. Brad and I had spoken to each other every day for three months, so it was going to be real hard having no contact for two whole weeks. He was so sweet and the night before I left, he biked down to my house and gave me a CD he'd made to take with me. I had a little cry after he'd left, I was going to miss him so much.

When I lay on the beach sunbathing, I'd smile to myself when Meatloaf or Metallica came on as it wasn't my kind of music at all, but it reminded me of him. Although it was a fab holiday, I got home sick, and the second week felt soo long.

The day before we left Ibiza, I went to a designer shop and bought Brad a t shirt, some aftershave, and a cap. I just wanted to get home to him now. My Mam and Dad had missed me and wanted to spend time with me, but I was young and in love, and all that was on my mind was meeting up with my boy, so I text him to tell him I was home.

I soon got back into the whole work routine again and decided after a few weeks that it was time to move on from my job at the hotel. I found a job at our local supermarket. It was ideal because I could walk to work, and the hours and pay were both good. I started off a shelf stacker and after a while I worked my way up to a supervisor working sixty hours a week over three different shops the community. I loved working with people, chatting to customers and was even happier when my bestie Kerry came to join me. We had such a laugh, especially when this lad came in one night asking us if we sold Johnny's. After we'd stopped blushing and he'd left we absolutely pissed ourselves.

There was this sweet little elderly lady, Ms. Spencer and she couldn't get to our shop, so she'd order a little delivery every week for it to be delivered. Every Thursday at 6 pm on the dot she'd ring up with her little order bless her. I'd then whizz around the shop and put everything in a trolley ready for the staff the next day. Every week I'd write her a little note with a kiss and a smiley face and pop it in her shopping bag. I welled up when she told me how much she loved that, it meant so much to me that it made her smile.

One afternoon it was my turn to make a brew and after many years my dad had led me to believe a tale of there was a *'man in the cash machine.'* I had no reason to believe anything other than this to be the truth. I thought it made perfect sense that behind that blue door sat a little man, with his flat cap on reading his paper was handing out money from the hole in the wall. I asked my boss Ted, quite confidently I might add, *"Does he want one in there do you think?"* Looking puzzled he said *"Erm, what? who you are talking about?"* Then he burst out laughing, no need for that I thought, I was only being polite. *"Oh, wow you actually think there's someone in there don't you?"* He asked as he looked at my straight face burning a bright red with humiliation. The penny finally dropped…that in fact this was not true. Cheers for that Daddio! *"There's no one in there is there?"* I cringed. He was still in hysterics and soon the story was spread over the supermarket. Funnily enough I recently popped into one of the stores and was met by one of my friends who still works there giggling, *"How scary, I was literally just talking about you and the man in the cash machine."* I'm glad I'm remembered for a reason that brings laughter to others because that's what life is all about.

I really looked up to older people, especially the ones I worked with. I loved spending time with them, listening to all their stories and advice on life. I soaked up everything they told me like a sponge, and I will forever call sweets… *'suckers.*

I worked with a lovely chap called George and a lady called Polly in the hardware store where we sold toys, electricals, and menswear. George took me under his wing and became like a second Dad to me. He'd call me *"Me ole mate,"* he always knew when I was down or upset and would know how to make me laugh. We'd sit together at tea break and put the world to rights. George was so funny everything had to be *his* way in *his* own time. If he was smashing up a box and saw a customer waiting at the till, he'd leave them waiting, and if they huffed and puffed, he'd make them wait longer. He was always getting told of by the manager.

At lunch Polly and me would sit together with our *'cup a soup'* and George would sit in his car listening to the cricket on his radio. Sometimes he'd nod off, so I'd end up tapping on the window of his car to wake him up before the dip shit of a manager came to find him and give him yet another bollocking. I just seemed to click with older people I don't know why I think it was because they made time for me and I felt safe around them, they also didn't judge me. The dick of a manager on the other hand was an absolute sleaze bag. He was so creepy and lazy but was one of those annoying people that would just so happen to be doing something constructive when the head office came to check in. I swear he must have had a radar that sensed he had to get up of his arse and do some work whenever they came around.

My Dad once came into the store looking for a new tv, I showed him to the manager's office so he could help him out. Seconds later dad came back to the counter laughing. *"Bugger the tv…get me a job here!"*

"Please don't tell me he is sleep again," I asked already knowing the answer.

It was so embarrassing. It was becoming a regular thing and soon his toothbrush appeared, so God only knows what he was playing at.

He would always be in my ear inviting me out clubbing with him, I kept telling him I wasn't interested, and, in the end, I had to literally tell him to fuck off. After a couple of months, he left so all was good.

Although I was happy and settled at work, I also wanted to do something about my education before it was too late. I was thankful of the experiences I'd gained in the outside world, but I felt it was the right time to apply for a place at college. After speaking to Ted about my decision he said he was happy for me to work shifts around my lessons which I was so grateful for as I was going to need bus fares every day.

I was so happy when I was accepted into college to study my A level's. I chose English, Law, Sociology and Psychology. I don't really know why I had gone for such complex subjects; other than the fact I was trying to prove I wasn't thick.

As my life was moving forward so was Nathan's. He'd formed a long-distance online relationship. He'd been to visit a few times and when she became pregnant, they planned their wedding in the UK. Personally, I thought it was all a bit quick, however that was none of my business and nor did I wish to make it so. I still didn't feel comfortable around him and imagine I never would. When the family got together the atmosphere was so awkward, they would sit huddled together in a corner whispering. It was so uncomfortable.

Around the same time another bombshell had hit the family as my sister Hollie had fell pregnant and her baby was due a few months apart. Hollie was just sixteen years old; she was just a baby herself and I worried about how she'd cope. It was a challenging time but also a happy one when her beautiful baby girl Isla was born in the summer as Nathan's baby boy was born a couple of months after.

Unfortunately, Hollie was living in a volatile relationship and true to my word I was there to support her and my baby niece as she went it alone as a single mam. I felt guilty that I wasn't going to be there for her as much as I wanted to, but I also couldn't wait to start my new adventure. I had the summer to prepare myself and jumped on the bus into town to buy all my new stationary and a backpack.

I was feeling so nervous when September arrived. This was a huge step for me, and I felt incredibly proud of myself for making the right choice for once. I wasn't going to know anyone, and I felt so shy around new people. Luckily, Brad was studying sports at the same college and reassured me he would meet me at breaktime to make sure I was okay.

My first lesson was English, and I made friends with a group of girls straight away. I just knew this was going to be different and it felt good.

I found College to be a completely different atmosphere to school, mainly because I was there as I wanted to learn and not because I was forced to. I loved Sociology, but I didn't like the debates and would blush if they encouraged me to join in, I hated confrontation of any kind so I would just listen. Psychology was my favourite subject. I learnt so much about behaviours, I also discovered things that related to my past and reasons as to why I coped with certain Situations and environments in the way I did. It helped me understand a lot about life.

I couldn't believe that I found myself 'enjoying' spending time in the

College library studying. (While also learning that if you logged on to MSN on the computers you could message your mates when you had run out of phone credit on your Nokia 3310).

The bus stopped just outside Brads house, so every morning I'd give him three rings on his mobile when we got to the bridge so he could literally roll out of bed and be at the bus stop in time, (lazy git). We would then walk hand in hand the half hour trek to college chatting about random shit, (well I would, he'd just listen). Every day we'd stop off at the corner shop for a scratch card each, and a bottle of blue top milk for Brad to down in one gob full for his breakfast.

As happy as I appeared to others, I was struggling with my confidence, and it was getting worse. I'd hide my petite frame underneath my *Adidas* trakkie bottoms and baggy T-shirt's. My friend asked me one day why I dressed like I did, hiding my figure. I'd always felt a great shame in my body, why the fuck would I want to show it off?

One summers day however, I thought I'd make more of an effort, so I wore a pair of beige fitted trousers and a tied front shirt. I couldn't accept the compliments and attention I attracted to myself, it made me feel too uncomfortable, so after that it was polos and trakkies all the way.

After a while Brad and I started arguing a lot, mainly due to my past. It just kept cropping up no matter how hard I tried to escape it. I was just constantly reminded that I was nothing but a slag with no hope.

The night before my 18 th birthday Brad broke up with me, leaving me inconsolable. It shouldn't have come as much of a shock as it was all too good to be true.

As the saying goes, *"If you love something set it free, if it comes back, it's yours, if it doesn't then it never was."*

I think because I was his first girlfriend it was maybe too much for him, which I completely understood. I gave him the space he needed, and I tried to move on and fix my broken heart, only this time it really was true love, so it hurt twice as much.

I woke up on my 18 th birthday feeling so empty. I pulled myself together and made my way downstairs to a pile of cards and presents waiting to be opened.

Daydreaming, I gazed out of the window of the bus, I didn't even notice Brad was on it until I saw him walking over and reluctantly passed me a present and card. Why he'd even bothered I don't know, being sure not to give me an ounce of hope, he muttered that he already brought it and walked off. The card was a very blunt scribble *From Brad*. I wasn't being ungrateful I just didn't see the point in it, all it'd done was leave me feeling confused and quite frankly ten times worse. I gave myself a talking to, I had to be strong and move on like an adult. Heartbreak is part of life and as grandpa had said I had to, *"Put it down to experience"* and move on. It wasn't like I hadn't done it before; my life had been full of hurt and starting overs.

Eventually I gained enough confidence to start going out again with my mates. we'd go cruising the streets in a little boy racer *VW Golf*. The speakers would be blaring with *Clubland* and *Creamfields* tunes, as we tucked into our Maccy Ds, Life was sound.

One night I'd got in late, I went to bed and fell straight to sleep. My phone then began to ring waking me up. The last person I thought it'd be was Brad. I honestly thought he was pissed up when he apologised and asked if I wanted to try again. Where had this come from? This was a first for me, never had a boy broken up with me and then regretted it after. I remained calm as I told him I would think about it, I wasn't going to bow down to him and why should I after how he had treated me, I had to show him some strength.

My Mam wasn't happy about it at first because she saw how much he'd hurt me. She told me that he wasn't welcome to the house either.

It wasn't ideal, but then in hindsight it made us more determined to make it work., right from the start our relationship had been challenged but this took it to the next level. We would now have to meet up in the chilly winter months, on a bench halfway up a hill between our houses.

Bless my Nanna Ava though, she liked Brad and she never judged anyone. She told us she didn't like us out in the cold in winter and that we were always welcome at her house. We never outstayed our welcome as the last thing we wanted was to cause trouble between her and my mum. Her acceptance was all the reassurance I needed.

I was always honest with my Mam and Dad, I never lied or sneaked around behind their backs to meet Brad either. They began to realise that it was serious between us, and it didn't matter what anyone said we would continue with our relationship regardless. God what a stubborn little mare was I?! and after nearly a year of meeting up at the same bench, my Mam and Dad gave up and welcomed him back into the family. With Brad and I both at college and work, and in between and his sports we didn't get to spend much time together, so his Mam suggested I stay over at weekends which I always looked forward to.

Brad and I have never been a couple to live in each other's pockets as we agreed that he had his own time and mates and I had mine. I guess looking back I could have been a little more supportive of him by watching him play footie, but then again, the one time I did go to one of his games, I made an absolute dick out of myself. I had absolutely no idea about cricket, I got bored, so I decided to go for a walk, as I walked round the edge of the big field in my own little world. I wondered what the big white board thing was as I stood looking at it. Then I heard Brad's voice shouting over at me. I thought how cute, so I waved back, then someone else waved and shouted, I thought that's a bit weird I don't know them. I then heard someone yell *"Get out the way of the bloody screen* ...Oh, that's what the big white thing was. It's safe to say that I didn't get asked to go and watch him again for a very long time.

My proudest moment had to have been when I went to watch him in the ring. He was in no doubt embarrassed (yet again) by my shouting and knocking over the chair behind me and then crying (obviously). I was so proud of him that I just wanted to burst.

I couldn't believe how quick my first year had gone in college and it was time to sit my exams. I had revised so hard for them so all that was left to do was hope and pray for the results I deserved.

My Mam and Dad were away on holiday and were waiting for my phone call. I went into the hall and picked up my envelope and walked outside to a bench where I sat on my own. I slowly opened the envelope, my heart was racing but it was a different feeling to getting my GCSE results, I didn't realise the importance of them, however this time I had chosen to learn and worked so hard for and was desperate for the results to reflect my efforts.

As I read the result my heart sank. Not only had I failed miserably I got a U. Yes, a U in one of my favourite subjects of Law. All this proved to me was that I was just as thick as I thought I was. What the hell was I even thinking trying to prove otherwise. I got an A and a B but because I failed one section the whole exam failed. How unfair is that? I couldn't believe my eyes at the F grade I'd got for English. I was completely devastated. I also got D in Sociology and Psychology.

As I walked away my tutor called to me to see if I was okay. After a chat I reluctantly agreed to go in and discuss my results with him. Apparently, the reason for my crap grades was because I had misread some of the questions.

After hearing that I just shut off to what else he had to say.

Enough was enough and made decision to walk away from education for good. It really wasn't worth all this disappointment, and I clearly wasn't cut out for it. Ted offered me back my full-time hours at work, which was blessing. Brad and I decided that together that we'd start saving up for our future whatever it may hold. I worked my butt off putting every penny I had spare aside.

"What you need is a bottom drawer duck" Nanna Ava told me. *"A bottom what?"* I laughed. *"A bottom drawer is a place where to keep things you buy for when you have your own house. It saves you a lot of money by getting bits and bobs every month rather than all in one go, so like coat hangers, tea towels, mugs, cutlery, anything you like."* What a fab idea. And

before long it wasn't just a bottom drawer, I had…it was more like a wardrobe, full of things for when we had our own home. I can't tell you how happy it made me feel inside. My pals would laugh at my bottom drawer/ wardrobe and how old fashioned it was. I tell you what though it's one of the best things I ever did. I didn't care what anyone thought anymore because finally I was looking forward and not back.

Heaven gains an angel

Late to the party as always … I decided that at nineteen, it was about time I learnt to drive. I was fed of relying on buses all the time, so I searched for a local driving instructor. I found a local chap, who tended to look a little on edge whenever I was in the driver's seat of his little blue Vauxhall Corsa. I felt nervous and uncomfortable during my lessons because of my insecurities, my confidence didn't seem to improve either, even after months of lessons. It was costing me a bomb and every lesson was becoming the same old bore. My friends had sailed through their tests, and there was me an absolute gibbering wreck.

The instructor seemed hesitant to let me drive on main roads as well, although in all fairness to him, it was understandable with the number of times he had to reach over and grab the steering wheel because I'd drifted over the road. Hmmm, and thinking about it I don't think it helped when he instructed me to turn right at the roundabout ahead, to which I immediately complied...literally turning right. Yeah, I guess that could have been a contributing factor for his decisions as to why he didn't feel too safe with me. I think he was perhaps relieved when I rang him to tell him I'd decided to take a break from lessons as I didn't feel I was ready. At the end of the day, I felt it like it was money that I could save for my future. I was taking up that poor instructor's time when there was someone else that was more deserving than I was.

A few months after I'd quit, Nathan announced that he was training to become a driving instructor. He asked me if I'd like to learn with him for a discounted price. My heart was saying yes but my head was screaming no. Why I agreed I don't know, I was desperate to pass my test and I was obviously still in denial about the abuse. I also felt sorry for him and felt pressured to support him and his new business. I arranged to have two lessons a week, in the hope that I would get through it and pass. Not that it worked out like that because five failed tests later, (yes you heard right by the way FIVE!) I was ready to cave in. I think a normal person would've given up out of embarrassment, but not me I picked myself up, brushed myself down and started all over again. I was trying so hard to be strong for my Nanna because she was sick at the time battling cancer for the third time. She was desperate for me to pass my driving test, I had to keep going for her to make her proud.

It was just after Christmas when Nanna gave us the news that the cancer was back for a third time. She had suffered in complete silence keeping it all to herself because she didn't want it to spoil our Christmas. That was my Nanna all over, always thinking of everybody else, no matter what she was she was going through, bless her beautiful soul. We promised her that as a family we'd climb the mountain together, reassuring her that she wasn't alone. The consultant said that the cancer was aggressive but also gave us the hope of chemotherapy but told us to be prepared for a long road ahead.

Some days Nanna would be so sick and on her better days she would live her life doing the things she loved the most like arts and crafts at the local hospice. Her diary soon became full yet again with hospital appointments, scans, tests, and treatment. She had fought this disease for five years and after the last time she proved herself to be a living, breathing miracle when she was so close to leaving us.

"I'm not ready to go just yet" she would say. *"Grampa came to me last night he wanted me to go with him… but I told him not just yet me duck."*

With tears rolling down my cheeks, it brought back the memories of when Grandpa came to me, so there was no doubt in my mind that it was true. Every day I would ask her, *"How are you feeling,"* the answer would always be the same, *"I'm ok sunbeam."*

But not that day.

"I'm tired. Tired of being asked if I am ok. What am I meant to say no I'm not ok I'm bloody dying?" It broke my heart that the cancer had sucked the absolute life out of her leaving her so weak and her once shiny beautiful peach skin was gradually turning yellow.

One afternoon we sat having a brew together when she kept drifting in and out of sleep, I knew in my heart that she was slowly giving up her fight. Not once over these five years of the pain and suffering she had endured had she complained.

The following week she was given the news that, *"The magic had worn off."*

Nanna Ava's wish was to spend her last days the same as Grandpa Jack had at home with everyone she loved by her side.

She had begged me not to cancel my fifth driving test, so the night before, I prayed the hardest that I had ever prayed before that I would be able to make her proud. The next thing I knew Nathan had rung to tell me he couldn't make it, even though it had scheduled for weeks. He kept making up excuses as to why he had to cancel. Instead of stressing out I just took a deep breath and told myself I'd be okay.

Luckily, I managed to find another instructor to take me to my test, however I was so worked up that with everything that had been going on that I put all my effort into impressing him in that one-hour lesson before than my actual test. I knew I'd failed before we even reached the test centre. It didn't help that there wasn't just one examiner but two of them, one of which coughed and spluttered for majority of the test in the back seat of the car. That was just my luck.

I looked at the examiners face, *"You don't have to say anything, I know."* I got out the car, stormed over to a nearby bin and kicked the crap out of it. I felt such a failure. I was dreading telling my Nanna, but when I did it wasn't me; she was disappointed in at all, it was Nathan. She just squeezed my hand and told me not to give up.

I tried so hard to make her smile just one last time as I sat by her bedside, I just found it hard to hold back my tears. In the end it was actually *her* that made *me* laugh. It must have taken all her strength when she turned to me, smiled, and said, *"I know that you've learnt how to make spaghetti Bolognese and as much as everyone likes it, they don't want it every night."*

A few days later Nanna peacefully passed away, in the same room and in the same bed as my grandpa, after thirteen years apart they were together at last. I'd just lost my best friend and I didn't know how I was going to be able to carry on without her by my side.

I finally plucked up the courage after a few weeks to take my test for the sixth and final time. I vowed not to put myself through it again so if I failed again, I'd be walking away. I was so ashamed of my previous failures that this time I didn't tell a soul about it.

It was hard to tell how I had done but I didn't hold out much hope as I pulled into the test centre carpark. I had my hand gripped to the door handle ready to exit. The examiner was straight faced and blunt, so I prepared myself for him to tell me I'd failed. When I heard the words … *"Ok, you've passed."* I literally couldn't believe it, *"Erm I'm sorry what, are you kidding me! are you sure?"* He looked blankly at me and repeated, *"You've passed,"* showing not an ounce of emotion. I don't think he quite realised what this meant to me. I was so excited my words raced out of my mouth without warning, *"oh I could kiss you," "Thank you, thank you, thank you so much."* I continued to ramble on.

"Please don't," he snapped as he handed me the papers, only this time it was *his* hand that was firmly gripped to the car door handle ready to make the sharp exit and not mine. He'd passed me because they were fed up with seeing my face at the test centre, not that I

gave a flying crap about that now because guess what?! I'd only gone and friggen done it!

FINALLY! I was so proud of myself for not giving up on one of the biggest achievements I'd ever made. It's only when you are met with challenges like this in your life that you sure feel grateful when something goes right for once, no matter how trivial it is. Its only now that I can see all the strength and sheer determination it must have taken for me to have learnt to deal with that failure repeatedly, and yet still be able to get back up and try again.

Brad already had a car as he just brought a truck for work, I'll never forget that pile of crap either. It was a little white Citroen Saxo, and it was a nightmare to drive. My arms felt like they'd done a triple biceps challenge at the gym. The worst part was driving up a multistorey carpark whilst trying not to roll back into the car behind because of its dodgy handbrake, but hey ho I had to be grateful, it was better than nothing.

Brad was working full time now as a builder and I felt ready to look for something more permanent. I knew working in a shop wasn't something that I wanted to do forever, I still wanted so desperately to be a nurse, but I knew I'd never be able to pass the exams, so I decided to apply for a carers position in a local nursing home. I was successful in my interview, but later I had a gut instinct something wasn't right, so I turned it down. When I heard that old saying, "All things happen for a reason," I never knew what it meant until one day it made sense...

Mam and Dad were having a conservatory fitted at the time when I got chatting to one of the builders one day, when my job came into the conversation. He told me that his wife worked in a private hospital and asked if I would be interested if there was anything available. Without hesitation I said, *"yes please, thank you so much."*

The next morning, I was just leaving for work when the builder arrived and handed me a business card, *"This is my wife Grace's number, she said there's one position still available, they tend to go pretty quick so give her a call if you're still interested."*

Nervously, I called the number on my mobile as I made my way up to work. Grace was so friendly and after a quick chat she said she would post out my application form and if asked if I could return it by the end of the week along with my CV., A week after I received a letter inviting me to an interview.

Because this was going to be my first proper interview, I wanted to make a good impression, so I picked out the smartest clothes I owned to wear. I glanced in the mirror as I left the house thinking, *"God I look like I'm going to a funeral."*

I arrived at the hospital about fifteen minutes early, good job as the interview was on the fourth floor, right at the top of the building.

Catching my breath, I pressed the buzzer and a friendly voice answered, *"Hi, are you here for the interview."*

"Yes," I replied so quietly she probably didn't hear me. The door clicked open and young girl in a smart nurse's uniform came down the corridor to meet me and point me in the direction of the visors room.

It didn't smell like a hospital at all, the floors were all carpeted, with beautiful pictures on the walls and fresh flowers in vases along the corridor, it was more like a hotel.

I heard my name being called so jumped up, reminding myself to smile be polite and say nothing that would later embarrass me. I knew that was going to be tricky. The two middle aged ladies wearing smart navy-blue nurses' uniforms, welcomed me into a little office. *"I'm Sister Jo, I'm the ward matron and this is Sister Lucie."* Sister Jo asked me to sit down and then looked down at her red clip board on her lap and began to ask me several questions about myself, and why I had applied for the position. I knew the dreaded question of 'what qualities do you have' been going to be making its appearance shortly… And yep, there it was.

'No, no, no, I hated this question.' So as if I were describing a car that was up for sale on a garage for court, I answered, *"Well, I'm reliable, loyal, trustworthy and I always try my best in what I do."*

They thanked me for attending the interview and as I stood up to walk out of the room, it felt was like someone was with me and gave me a push of courage as I blurted out, *"I just love to be around people, and I love to make others smile and feel special. I feel that by having experienced and learned to deal with illness, sadness and grief, If I were given the opportunity to be able to comfort and reassure someone by genuinely understanding what they are going through, would mean so much more to them than anything else."* Holy crap! where did that come from.

They looked at each other and smiled and asked me to wait back in the visitor's room. After about fifteen minutes they returned, Sister Jo smiled and said, *"We would be so pleased if you would join our ward as a Nursing assistant."* I could have cried, in fact I'm pretty sure I did cry. Not that it'll come as a surprise, as by now you've read half my life story and know that it's my natural response to almost anything and everything.

I couldn't wait to tell everyone my news, I was so excited.

The following week Sister Jo rang me to arrange for me to collect my uniforms, ID badge and paperwork. As she passed me the paperwork to sign, she looked down, *"Good heavens, what on earth has happened to your hands?"* Thinking very carefully before answering, oh shit fake tan that's what happened that's what.

"Oh, erm, I forgot to wear gloves." I blushed. *"Oh, you must be more careful."* She laughed, she then led me to the nurse's station to meet the rest of the staff on duty. Everyone was so friendly and welcoming. I left the hospital ward with a warm and happy feeling inside, I was sure that it'd been sent to me at the right time, maybe it was my beautiful Nanna watching over me.

My last day at the shop was full of hugs and tears, I really was going to miss them all. Ted gave me the most gorgeous good luck card signed with messages from everyone. He then handed me a beautifully wrapped gift box, as I opened it, I just couldn't believe the thoughtfulness and generosity of every one of them. Inside the gift box was the most beautiful, shiniest nurses fob watch. I was going to wear it on my uniform with such pride. Wiping away my tears, I handed over my keys along with my hideous overall dress thingy, that I wasn't going to miss, and I walked out of the squeaky doors.

I had a week to chill out and prepare myself for my new job.

My first shift at the hospital was a late shift, so my morning was spent laying in the bath until the water turned cold, my head was full of self-doubt that nobody would like me.

I pulled up my new M&S thick black tights, zipped up my smart blue dress and clipped up my belt. I put on a little mascara and lippy and I then pinned on my shiny fob watch above my name badge.

I was bursting with pride for the first time in a long while. I'd finally turned a corner; things were looking up and it felt amazing…

For Nanna and Grandpa – 2004

My angels in the sky

You never really left me

You were just too precious to stay

You didn't deserve all that suffering and

I'm so thankful now that you are free

To spread your angel wings in sky so bright

And though my tears will continue to fall and

I can no longer feel your physical warm embrace

I can hear you whisper in my ear

That your forever there to love and guide me

For the most precious gift of all…

Is to be able to call you, my angels in sky.

The magic of new beginnings

"You don't need a lot of money, but you also need to be comfortable."

Nanna Ava always gave the best advice. Both my Grandparents had worked hard for everything they owned, not tight as such, but always sensible. They believed that you shouldn't live beyond your means and if you couldn't afford something then you'd learn to be patient and wait until you could. As I got older Nanna Ava told me that were two most important things that I should invest in one was a reliable car (glad someone had faith in me) and the second was a house.

Brad and I had been together for four years when we felt the time was right to search for our first ever home and after a lot of saving, we had enough money to put down as a deposit on a house. We'd decided that it'd be more beneficial to get ourselves on the property ladder rather than waste money on renting, so we booked an appointment with a mortgage adviser before we started looking.

After receiving a list of properties from the estate agents, we ended up putting an offer in on the first house we viewed, it was a beautiful little two-bedroom terraced house with a cottage feel about it. There wasn't a garden but there was a shared courtyard with enough room for a washing line and a few flowerpots. We didn't care that we didn't have a working tv or brand-new furniture to move in with, we were just happy that we had a new adventure ahead of us.

Moving into our home together was the turning point in my life that I'd been waiting for and I felt content and positive about our future.

I loved anything to do with being creative so was in my element when I could choose and design my own on décor. Every spare minute I had would be spent with my tunes on, wallpapering, painting, and assembling Ikea furniture. Brad would often go off to Cricket on a Saturday morning and come home to a different coloured front room.

Thankfully, we lived in a nice, quiet area with friendly neighbours. We became close friends with Rosa, the lady two doors down. We could chat for hours, and she became a special part of our family. When we first met Rosa, I'm not sure why but she insisted on calling me the wrong name, but it stuck so I went along with it. What's worse, I even put it as my name in her Christmas card! I don't know who felt more embarrassed me or her, when I finally gave in and admitted that my name wasn't Emma. Luckily, she saw the funny side of it. Why I never told her I don't know but that's just what I'm like. It wasn't even the first time it happened… a girl at work in the canteen did the same thing. I just smiled and wave when I heard her call me Danielle... for like three years! She only found out my real name because a friend of my Mam's came into the canteen and heard her when she hollered over at the top of her voice, *"What did you call her? Danielle, what the?? That's not her name… I used to bite her bum when she was baby, I should know."* Now that was awks.

Rumour has it that you gain weight when you're in love… well I think that I'm living proof that it does! I'd completely let myself go and even though I went to aerobics classes and swam twice a week Brad and I sure as hell ate a lot of crap. Mondays were '*Soaps night*' where we would be in bed by seven and would binge watch *Easties* and *Corrie* while we smashed a bag of cheese and red onion sensations, *Cadbury's* dairy milk chocolate and a pack of suckers.

(Wine gums.)

I knew I was eating more than I ever had before, but I didn't realise that I was also psychologically building a protective barrier around me by using comfort food as a crutch.

I was sitting on the sofa one afternoon in a bikini top when Brad walked in and laughed,

"Alright tubs." I felt so ashamed because for the first time in my life I was content with my body, I hadn't even noticed that I'd put weight on, in fact it was the first time I'd ever gained any weight. I knew he didn't mean anything by it, but it was too late because it was a sore subject. I went upstairs and covered myself up and swore I'd never wear a crop top ever again. I didn't blame Brad, he had no idea what I had been through over the years with my body confidence and weight issues and is still oblivious, unless he reads this, because I don't think he would have said if he'd have known.

Between my shifts I tried to keep as active as I could, and I was determined to keep to a healthy weight in a sensible way. I pushed the urge to binge, use laxatives or make myself sick to the back of my mind.

Anyone who works shifts whether it be nursing, or any other job will know just how hard it is to maintain a balance of a healthy diet in between twelve-hour shifts, especially where there is the temptation of chocolates and biccy's in reach to pick at on the ward. As well as chips covered in gravy and sponge pudding with thick custard in the canteen.

Life was busy with keeping a home and a job, Brad and I didn't get to spend a great deal of time together, especially if I was on a ten-day stint at work. Brad worked on a building site in the week and did private jobs at a weekend and when he wasn't at work, he played sports. Although it was tough, we got used to it and made it work. Socially it didn't really bother us as I'd always had my space and time with my friends, and he had his.

I couldn't believe how quick the time had passed and the months had suddenly turned into years. I'd also managed to save up enough money to buy my own car. I fell in love with a baby blue Peugeot 306. I felt Nanna Ava and Grandpa Jack watching over me *"I've done it!"* I whispered to them. A house and a car, I wasn't even twenty-one yet.

Three years on and I still loved my job just as much as did at the start. I had gained a wealth of experience in the private hospital, and I'd passed my NVQ'S in health and social care. I learnt to deal with so many different areas of nursing too, whether a patient needed a hip or knee replacement, had suffered a sports injury, or sadly had cancer. Whatever the reason that brought them into the hospital, I'd do all I could to make them as comfortable as they could be. Every patient was a 'someone,' a parent, a child, a grandparent, a brother, sister, or an aunt and that's just how they deserved to be cared for. It was hard not to get close to a select few patients, especially when it was in my nature, and I'd formed a bond with them. I remember a lovely lady, who was heartbreakingly at the end of her life. The scent of the most beautiful flowers overwhelmed me as I quietly opened the door to check in on her one afternoon. The room had a slight chill in the air while at the same time a feeling of calm surrounded her as '*Frank Sinatra's Fly me to the moon,*' was playing low on a CD player at her bedside. Love her heart I hope she's in peace now.

At the end of a shift, I'd check the rota to see who I'd be working with the next day, don't get me wrong I loved working with everyone just some more than others. It was such an emotionally and physically draining job, working a shift with a good team beside you made all the difference to how you coped. I was so lucky to have made the closest friends, that I still have by my side today. We'd go out for dinner after shifts and clubbing at the weekends. Three of us had such a laugh and called ourselves, *'The pink ladies'* from the movie *'Grease.'*

There was never a dull moment, which would normally lead to me catching the most uncontrollable giggles at handover, especially when I was collecting the patient's dinner trays one afternoon. So, there I was with my hands full of heavy trays making my way down the corridor. As I got closer to the kitchen, I tried to walk faster because I could feel my stocking slipping down my leg, by time I reached the nurses station it was round my ankle. Hoping no one had noticed I quickly threw the trays on the side and pulled it back up. When I walked back on to the ward the girls were stood there peeing their pants. It wasn't all laughs, there'd be days that I'd be driving home in tears, you just never knew what sort of shift you we were going to have, but that's just how it was.

All I did know was that this was one of the happiest and most settled
I'd felt in a long while... but as the good old saying goes,

"All good things must come to an end." It was like I wasn't allowed to feel happiness, and if I did it would either be taken away or challenged. Once again Bruce the big black cloud had managed to find me...

I felt overwhelmed with so many emotions. One minute I'd get a rush of excitement the next I would feel so low that I felt I couldn't cope with life. I'd be overpowered with feelings of anger so much so that I'd throw just about anything that was in my reach. I lost count of the number of things I broke by lobbing them across a room, we got through a fair few TV flickers and phones, I know that much. I'd get so frustrated and the only way I felt I could release my anger was to express it through violence for some reason. I hated myself so much and felt ashamed of how bad my destructive behaviour had become. I just wanted it all to stop, and it'd be best if I weren't here anymore. I wanted to erase the strong emotions going around in my head once and for all...

I lay in the bath staring at the ceiling. My head hurt, and my eyes stung as I fought the tears. I gazed down at the razor in my hand shaking as I slowly moved it towards my wrist. A sharp scratch, a trickle of red blood and a feeling of relief. I shut my eyes and took a few deep breaths. Knock, knock, knock. I could hear a loud banging in the distance. *"Who the fuck is that."* My heart raced as I sat up in the bath and fell back in that present moment. I hugged my knees to my chest and sobbed loudly. Wiping my face with the Lukewarm soapy water, I stepped out of the tub and wrapped a towel around my shivering body. I looked through the gap in the curtains, whoever it was had gone now. I sat on the bed thinking about what had just happened. '*What was happening to me?*' I shouldn't be feeling like this. I had to pull myself together. I had a loving family and friends, I was in a stable relationship, and I loved my job, yet I was full of emptiness and sadness. I felt so guilty for feeling this way as memories of the past were consuming my mind.

I saw the doctor and he suggested to have a break from the pill I was on because it could be contributing to mood swings. I did what he suggested, I also decided to keep a diary of how I was feeling.

Three times a week after our shift my friend Faith and I would go swimming. One week I struggled to swim my normal fifty lengths and got out before her. On the way home I told her that I hadn't been feeling well. The first thing she asked me was, *"You're not pregnant, are you?"* Shit, I'd not even thought of that, I'd only been off the pill a month so I couldn't possibly be pregnant. Faith encouraged me to do a test to put my mind at rest. She dropped me off at home and I went

straight to the chemist around the corner where I bought a pack of two tests. Right well that reads one line ok ...that's a negative then. I must just be late on my period or something. As I chucked the test in the bin, I looked at it again and noticed there was a cross in the little window. WTF?! I ran back upstirs to the loo and did the second test. Clear as day it was positive. Oh, my days. I was in shock, but a good shock if that makes sense. Straight away I rang Faith and told her. She was so happy for us. I then got in my car and drove to my Mams; I could feel the clamminess of my palms slipping on steering wheel. I hadn't even told Brad yet as I wanted it to be a surprise for when he got home from work. I ran down Mam and Dads drive and into the house...
"I'm having a baby!" I cried and laughed at the same time. She was so happy; we had a quick

brew together to calm me down and then I went back home to wait for Brad. My heart was thumping through my chest as I paced up and down in the kitchen waiting for him. In he comes, kicks off his muddy boots, throws his backpack on the floor and looks over at me dancing around and beaming like a Cheshire cat. *"Guess what?"* I ask him, *"Erm what?"* he smiled... *"We're having a baby!"* I cried (again), as I gave him the positive pregnancy tests.

We stood in the kitchen hugging for which seemed like forever.

I don't think the reality really hit me until I was sat in the waiting room for the Midwife appointment. Coincidentally, I recognised her from the hospital, so it was nice to see a friendly face. Carrie told me how the first twelve weeks were most important, *"Lots of self-care and avoid heavy lifting."* I laughed as she knew as well as I did how hard that was going to be. I decided to tell Sister Jo and my close friends early on as I didn't want them to think I was being lazy. Or should I say I kind of just blurted out … *"I'm gonna be a Muma."* Needless to say, I did end up with a few bollockings off sister Jo if she caught me lifting a patient or moving something heavy. I wasn't used to being mollycoddled so it felt weird.

I loved growing a baby and even named my bump, *"Baby monkey,"* I'd talk and sing to him/ her all the time while stroking my little bump. (Yep, I was one of those Baby Mama's who constantly stroked her belly.)

I ended up being referred to a consultant as the midwife was slightly concerned about how narrow my pelvis was. (Basically, I may not be able to push this watermelon out of my tiny vag) I cringed as he added *"Oh and I'll write on your notes that the labour shouldn't exceed ten hours, ok?"* … Shit the bed, this was happening.

Now prepare yourself with the Kleenex for what comes next is so romantic that it would give a romantic engagement proposal in the Maldives a run for its money ….

Only kidding…

We had just got in to bed, well I had rolled, and Brad had elegantly placed himself on the bed when he asked me, *"Do you we think we should get married before the baby arrives, so we all have the same name?"*

"Erm Yeah I guess so," I yawned.

"Well tomorrow we'll go to see your mam and dad, I want to ask your dads permission as its tradition." He went on, to which I simply replied with,

"Ok! Night," and grunted off to the land of nod.

Yeah, I guess you could say that I've always been the dreamer and he's more of the practical type.

As planned the next day after work we made our way to my parents' house, they were happy for us and offered to help as much as they could with the planning of our special day.

We didn't feel the need for a big do, so we searched up a local registry, but before I rang, we had a date in mind. I felt sad that there would be an empty seat where Nanna Ava should be, so we decided on the 5th of November as that was her birthday. It'd be our way of including her in our special day. We just had to hope it was available at such short notice. The lady confirmed that it was all booked in for November 5th, 2005, at 3 pm.

With seven weeks to go we had our work cut out.

Luckily, there was a bridal shop in our village that had been there for years, I remember when I was a little girl, I'd walk past and gaze at all the beautiful white dresses in the big windows, in the hope that one day I would be someone's bride, and now that day had come.

When I stepped into the shop for the first time, it was just as I imagined it to be, full of the most stunning dresses, shoes, and jewellery that I'd ever seen. The shop assistant clocked my baby bump and offered a variety of dresses to try on that could be altered weekly if needed before the day. The first dress I tried on was gorgeous, but it just didn't look right on a short fat person, the second one was stunning but a little too lacy, but the third was just perfect. It was a simple but beautiful ivory gown, with tiny diamanté details. The lady then showed my Mam how to tie the long train up at the back of the dress up into a bow, for the evening reception. I chose a beautiful lace veil, crystal tiara and a pair of silk ivory shoes. I was about to leave the shop when I noticed the most gorgeous jewellery sets in a glass cabinet. I really wanted something special for Hollie and my little niece Isla as they were my bridesmaids, so I chose Hollie a pale pink crystal necklace and earrings set to match her dress and Isla a little silver cross.

Our big day had arrived, and I was about to leave for my Mam's to get ready when the door knocked. It was Brad's Mum; she was so excited and told me before I left to pack an overnight bag because they'd booked a surprise for us. I was speechless! I ran upstairs and blew the dust off my holdall from on top of the wardrobe and packed it with my jammy's and toiletries. We felt so blessed to have such a supportive family around us helping us arrange everything with such little time and the seven weeks soon passed.

The ceremony wasn't until 3 pm so we had ample time to get ready. I stood in the bathroom and did my make up as I did, I said a little prayer asking for everything to go to plan. We had a few tears before mum left for the registry office. I sat in my wedding dress on the sofa staring into space when dad came in, *"c'mon love let's go."* I then heard a car horn beep *"Who's that?"* I asked him. *"It's your lift"* he said smiling. *"But I thought you were driving…"*

Outside the front of the house was a vintage Aston Martin decorated with flowers and bows. I burst into tears; I wasn't expecting that, it was such a lovely surprise. I was shaking with nerves when dad put his arm round my shoulder, *"You're ok love."* I could always rely on him to help me feel at ease. I felt so emotional because for twenty years my dad had looked after me and now, he was going to be giving me away to the man I would be spending the rest of my life with.

As we stopped at the registry office the chauffer held open the door when my dress decided to get stuck, dress stuck between dad was too busy admiring the car and talking to the driver to notice, (God he was just like me chopsin' to everyone.) I eventually set myself free without ripping my dress and with a deep breath I took my dad's arm… there was no turning back, not literally there was no turning back as we got stuck in the friggen doorway, I think I must have underestimated just how big I'd gotten. I don't even think anyone noticed as they were all too busy watching themselves being recorded or the large screen in the corner of the room, while listening to *Vivaldi*.

The ceremony was lovely, well other than another moment when I struggled to put the ring on Brad's finger. The photographer joked *"Try not to drawer blood!"* Oh, and then Brad had forgotten what my full name as we made our promises to each other. I'd asked one of my close friends to read one of my favourite readings by *'Stephen Curtis Chapman,'* called, *'I will be here.'* I'm so glad that I had shoved that emergency tissue down my bra...

My Auntie Lydie's wedding gift to us was to be our photographer,

"Look this way, now the other way... now say sex," She was so funny. Brad didn't like weddings at the best of times, so it was a bit of a challenge to get him to crack a smile, (looking at our photo's you'd think I'd dragged him there against his will) Auntie Lydie did capture a beautiful picture of me looking down as my friend held her hand on my bump, I just love that photo. I was knackered and I still had the reception to get through yet! We arrived at the country pub and the driver opened the car door, it was so windy that I sort of blew out of the car with my veil blowing across my face, smearing my lipstick. I must have looked like I'd been yanked through a hedge backwards when Brad and I emerged from the car into the pub and made our way to the reception room.

Speechless we couldn't believe the effort our families had gone to, it was beautiful. Mam had even managed to have a gorgeous cake made in secret. I looked around the room at the stunning flower arrangements and balloons. I felt so blessed and couldn't believe that this was all done for us. After the meal, my dad stood up to do his speech, beforehand he had made a promise to me that he wouldn't embarrass me, and he wouldn't make me cry.

He did both.

"If you want a marriage to last" he began…

"Then my son in law is the perfect example…you will be that busy with work and sports that you won't get to spend enough time together to argue!"

He did make us laugh bless him. That had always been our family's way of dealing with the struggles of life, to just make jokes, after all laughter is the best medicine.

Our first dance was to our song, *"There you'll be"* by *Faith Hill,* it's always been a special song for us, and always will be.

I was then so busy dancing the night away with my friends and family and making sure I had spoken to everyone to thank them for coming, that I didn't even see the buffet let alone taste it. Just when we thought the day couldn't get any better, my Mam appeared on the stage dressed up as a cowgirl with blonde wig and started singing *"Stand by your man."* My Mam doesn't even drink, so it must have taken some guts for her to have done that.

I know this sounds all very lovely, doesn't it? I'll give you the honest version now because not everything went as smoothly as planned and my wedding day actually consisted of …

My hairdresser arriving an hour and half late bless her, stick on nails that refused to stay put, and a huge hoop under my dress that kept slipping down, due to seven-month preggers bump! Our jaws ached from all the smiling, and even if it did take three of us in bog to hold my dress up, it was our kind of perfect.

By ten o clock *I'd had me chips*, as Mam would say and was tired. A taxi was waiting outside for us and drove us through the countryside to a beautiful hotel in a little village. A lovely couple greeted us at the entrance and showed us to our gorgeous room. After stuffing my face with the complimentary chocolates, I collapsed onto bed.

The next morning, we sat on the balcony with a brew, it was so peaceful listening to the birds singing and the views were incredible.

Our honeymoon on the other hand, (without sounding ungrateful) was the complete opposite. As you can imagine how cold it would be in the month of November, (well let me tell you it was perishing). I sat next to Brad on the most uncomfortable camping chair, wrapped up tightly in a blanket freezing my tits off, so no we didn't go to Maldives, wait for it... We went fishing. Yep fishing!! I mean every girl's dream, right? I bet you are all well jel now, aren't you? I was still trying to warm up three days later.

We had so much more now look forward and this was just the start of our new adventure...

I will be here – by Stephen Curtis Chapman

Tomorrow morning if you wake up and the sun does not appear

I will be here

If in the dark we lose sight of love, hold my hand, and have no fear

I will be here

When you feel like being quiet or when you want to speak your mind, I will listen

I will be here when the laughter turns to cryin'
Through the winning, losing and tryin' we'll be cause

 I will be here

Tomorrow morning if you wake up and the future is unclear

I will be here

As sure as seasons are made for change Our lifetimes are made for years so

I will be here

I will be here, and you can cry on my shoulder when the mirror tells us were older

I will hold you to watch you grow in beauty and tell you all the things you are to me

I will be here

I will be true to the promise I have made to you and to the one who gave you to me

I will be here

Blessed mama

 I hoped to be the 'perfect Mama,' who always looked fab while her children were pristine and well behaved.
Not me …I was the Mam who pushed five days in with dry shampoo, baggy clothes to hide my bulges, along with the trademark toothpaste smeared down the front of my t-shirt, sick on my shoulder and chocolate biscuit crumbs around my calves from the grubby fingers that clung to my legs when I washed up. The struggle was real I tell you.

I've always had such high expectations of myself, knowing deep down that I'd probably fail and then beat myself up for not being good enough, or even worse 'perfect.' Instead, what I've learnt is that we're all winging   at life, strolling down our own paths at our own pace, it doesn't matter how fast or slow or even successful our journey is, what matters the most is that we have love in our hearts, happiness in our souls and that we show kindness to ourselves and others. Wouldn't the world be a better place if we all did this? Like many others, Ive had to accept that not everyone feels the same way that I do, and I swear that some people are just put on earth to challenge our strength by pissing us off, but that's ok, because that's what make us who we are today. Not everyone is as thankful or grateful as I am, and do you know what? I feel so sad for them. They may never get to feel any kind of love for themselves or anyone else, so rather than let that type of person affect our own feelings and beliefs, we must learn to blow their negative energy away, replacing it with love and light because that's all they really need. Kindness costs nothing. Can you imagine living a life full of hate and judgement? I know that it makes me feel bad just thinking about it. One of life's most important lessons is that we don't judge each other, no one is perfect…

So, this is to all you beautiful Mama's, who I so wrongly criticised in Sainsbury's as your little ones screeched their heads off in the trolley. I can't apologise enough for my pure ignorance. I honestly believed that my child would never behave in such a way, I also thought that I would produce a perfect one. This was naive of me, I truly am sorry, please forgive me. Ironically, my daughters first paddy was at the checkout in a supermarket, trying to pry the Peppa pig book from her grip, it didn't help that the grumpy old granny behind me stood tutting and glaring at us.

What I wanted to scream was '*fuck you*' but instead I did the whole, "*Come on Nyla, let Mammy pay the lady with the pennies for your book, then you can have it right back.*" Did it work? Did it buggery! And yes, it would have been easy to give in to her, instead I stood firm and saved the tears for the walk back to the car. I pushed the pram with one hand while holding my screaming toddler with the other. So yeah, like I said ironic…I was now *that* Mam with the kiddo throwing a paddy.

I'm sure baby monkey had waited for me to squeeze into my wedding dress to have a huge growth spurt, I ballooned up a mahoosive four stone by the end of the pregnancy, the girls at work had to cut the pleats out the back of my uniforms to allow room for my forever growing belly. My friends would say, *"Oh your glowing,"* *but* I knew I looked like the *Michelin man* from the tyre advert.

It was a bittersweet moment as I waddled off the ward to start my maternity leave, I was excited for the future, but was already worrying about how I'd cope with returning to work after having a baby.

Since we didn't know what we were expecting, we'd decided to decorate the nursery in pastel greens and lemons. I'd chosen a

'*Classic Winnie the Pooh*' style themed wallpaper, with bedding and Curtains to match. We had a beautiful navy blue Britax pram, and a white embroidered Moses basket all set up ready for baby monkeys' arrival, as well as stacks of nappies and baby wipes. I'd spend hours in the nursery, daydreaming about what my baby would be like, folding the tiny white vests and Babygro's. I couldn't help but sniff the sweet scent of *fairy* washing powder as I neatly placed them in the drawers. *Marie Kondo* style of course.

The week before my due date Brad and I received a letter from the hospital, inviting us for a tour of the labour ward. I guess the idea was to reassure us, however for me it had the complete opposite effect. We sat in silence in the car on the way to my Mam and Dad's. My mind was going overtime, as soon as we walked in their front door, I broke down, *"I can't do it, I can't push a baby out and I can't be a mam."*

The truth was I was shitting myself; it didn't help that the familiar voice was in my head telling me I was bound to fail.

No matter how much you think you are prepared or believe you know what you are doing, nothing can prepare you for motherhood. There's no instruction manual, so you have to guess your way through it. I had all these hopes and dreams about what it was going to be like, naively I thought the baby would pop out and sleep, feed, play and look cute. Let's just say I had a lot to learn. *"It's just like taking a big pooh,"* my friend said laughing. *"Honestly, no big deal, if it hurt that many women wouldn't keep doing it."* That's true, I thought. A

big pooh, yeah, I can do that, no problemo…
I'd be just fine and dandy.

I was beginning to feel really fed up and
frustrated, as baby monkey's due date came
and went, I spent the following nine days
answering messages and calls repeating the
same answer, to same question, *"Have you not
had that baby yet?" Ahrrrrrrgh.*

Until finally …

It was the 20 th of February 2006, I couldn't
settle or sleep so we watched *Nil by Mouth* on
the DVD player in bed, hoping that I'd drop
off, I don't think anyone would be able to
drop off to that film though to be fair, (it's a
movie full of smashing each other about, drugs
and booze.) I tossed and turned all night until I
suddenly felt the urge to get up and go to the
loo, as I stood up it was like someone had

turned a tap on full stream as gushes of water ran down my legs. I rang Mam to tell her what had happened. *"It's ok it sounds like your waters have broken, ring the labour ward and they'll tell you what to do."*

Finally, a nurse answered the phone and told me to go into labour ward to be checked over. Carefully, I stepped over the puddles of water across the kitchen tiles and went up to have a shower, I was in labour but all I could think about was my greasy barnet.

My bump felt heavy, my back ached, and my legs were sore from the leaking water rubbing against my skin, (which had started to look like I had an undeniable incontinence problem.) I was shown to a bay of other women in labour and an hour later a midwife came to examine me. She told me that I was only 2 cm dilated and to go home until my contractions felt stronger. The midwife suggested I take a warm bath and relax as much as I could. I thought it was a bit weird myself, but I trusted them.

Mam was also my birthing partner, so it made sense for us to stay together until it was time to go back into hospital, so we went straight to their house. I had a soak in the bath like they suggested, hoping it'd ease the pain a little, but soon the contractions were that strong that I was clinging onto the edge of the bathtub. My contractions were getting stronger and closer together, so we made our way back to the hospital…

Cut a long story short, as it wasn't the most glam, I was in labour for over twenty-six hours, with a mix of…bouncing on a big blue birthing ball, high on gas in air, copious amounts of pethidine, laying in a birthing pool wondering why they kept ignoring me when I repeatedly asked for Radox bubble bath, while watching my hot pink nail polish float on the top of the water. After all that, I agreed to an epidural, which was bliss because I couldn't feel a thing. I was exhausted. *"Why the fuck did Eve eat the apple off the tree?"* I screamed. *"Erm, I dunno!"* Brad answered, looking worried. *"No, well I'll tell you why, because Adam was nothing but a bastard."* I didn't know what the frig I was saying, but I do remember shouting repeatedly, *"I'm being loud aren't I," "I'm loud, I really am, oh I'm sorry I'm loud!"* (I don't think they dare tell me how loud I actually was, until after the birth.) When I was conscious, I could see Brad was nodding off on a bed of coats on the floor and Mam was sitting next to me looking concerned. She didn't have to say anything, I just knew something wasn't right. The next thing I knew three midwifes and a doctor were gathered around my bed looking even more worried. *"What's wrong, what's happening?"* I asked. The Doc explained that my baby's head was stuck, and the heart rate was high, which suggested the baby was distressed. *"We need to get your baby out, NOW."* That Doc saved both mine and my baby's life. The next thing I knew I was squiggling my signature at the bottom of a consent form, for an emergency caesarean section. I was filled with both worry and relief all at the same time. Everything after that was a blur, I lay looking up at the bright white lights flickering above me as we passed through the empty corridors. I was petrified as the midwives' pushed me on a bed through the operating theatre doors. I was worried about Mam as well, she suffered with severe anxiety and agoraphobia. I felt so sad for her that she had been by my side through the whole labour, and now she was going to miss the most important part.

After about twenty minutes the Nurse said that my baby had been born. *"What's happening."* *"Why's my baby not crying?"* I could see them all gathered round a little crib, eventually a nurse came over, *"You have a baby girl; she is having difficulty breathing so she's going to have to be taken down to the special care unit. Do you have a name for her?"*

"Yes, Nyla," I cried, and with that they wrote her name tag, and she was gone.

I must have fallen asleep because the next thing I remember was waking up on a ward. Mam then came in; the hospital staff hadn't told her anything bless her. *"Are you ok, where's the baby?"* Bursting into tears I told her, *"All I know is that I've had a girl and she's in special care, I don't even know what she weighs or looks like, and we've named her Nyla."*

A nurse came over to us and explained that Nyla had been taken to the special care baby unit. She had to stay in an incubator because she had an infection from the traumatic birth. She told Brad and Mam that they could see baby Nyla, I however had to wait until later due to the surgery. Mam was reluctant to as she knew how upset I was, but I reassured her it was fine, and I wanted her to meet her baby grand daughter. I lay thinking about her, hoping and praying that she'd be ok, when my friend popped up to see me. She worked in the hospital and was on her way to work, she had bought me the cutest 'baby monkey!' teddy. It was so thoughtful of her; I held on to him so tight and fell back to sleep. I was woken up to Brad opening the curtains around my bed…

"I couldn't resist," he beamed as he handed me a bag of the most gorgeous pink Babygro's and vests, bless him. He had been truly amazing, I couldn't have coped without him, feeling the strongest love for him right now, more than ever before.

It wasn't until nine o'clock at night when a nurse headed over to me with a wheelchair. *"You can go down to special care now."* Looking down at the wheelchair I snapped, *"I don't need that thing,"* but the nurse insisted I use it, reminding me that I'd had major surgery and still had a catheter I had in. Reluctantly I let Brad wheel me down to meet my baby girl. The first thing that struck me was her beautiful hair, it was so long and a gorgeous blend of blondes, browns, and auburn, *"It looks like she's got highlights!"* The nurse came over and told me that Nyla had found her voice and that it was a good sign. I then kissed my finger and stroked her tiny hand through the hole in the incubator, *"goodnight baby girl."* I knew it was time for Brad to leave, I really didn't want to be on my own. I held him tight, and he promised to text me when he was home.

Back on the ward I managed to have a little freshen up; I was adamant the catheter was going to be removed and I was going to walk the next day. True to my word, the next morning I was able to walk around the bed and my catheter was removed. By evening, I was doing laps up and down the ward. I was feeling stronger by the hour, and I wasn't one for lazing around, I was determined this wasn't going to hold me back, I had to be strong for my baby girl. Later, that morning I found myself sitting in a room which felt more like a small closet, on a chair that looked about a hundred years old. My boobs were firmly hooked up to what I can only describe as a huge, cold, stainless steel, milking machine.

"You need to pump as much as you can." The nurse snapped as she also somehow managed to squeeze into the tiny room. It was pure agony, I told her I couldn't do anymore, reluctantly she told me I could see Nyla. I had gotten used to the high pitch sound of Nyla's cry when walking into the special care baby unit, probably because she was the only baby that cried as loud as she did. The nurses encouraged me to keep going back down for feed times to encourage her into a routine, however I found myself avoiding spending time with

her. Every time I held her, she cried, and I'd started to feel detached from her. I spent more time on the ward than with my new baby. I was crying one minute and laughing the next. I spent the evenings looking after the other new Mams. I'd make them tea and biscuits to keep their strength up, completely forgetting the fact that I too was a new Mam.

Brad on the other hand was a natural, he cared for Nyla so well. He fed her and changed her nappies, each time describing her poo to me and what each colour meant. I wasn't interested one bit. Unbeknown to me, mum and the nurses had been discussing my behaviour towards Nyla because they were concerned, they tried to talk to me, but nothing made sense, I'd sit and watch the other Mams with their babies, I knew something didn't feel right. I honestly felt she didn't like me. Every time I'd walk into special care, I heard her before I saw her, why didn't the other babies cry like this? *"Yes, finally here's mammy!"* the nurses said pushing her round and round in a pram, or she'd be over someone's shoulder behind the nurse's station, 'Baby monkey' was the right name for her!

After a long seven days the consultant said he was satisfied with Nyla's progress and agreed for us to finally go home.

The night before we came home, I made a conscious effort to see Nyla before I went to sleep. I picked her up out of her crib, I held her close and walked around the room with her. It was so silent. *"Mammy and daddy love you so much, we will always be here for you, everything is going to be just ok.*" I whispered to her. Gently, I lowered her into her crib. The next morning, I got up early, excited to be going home.

Breathing a sigh of relief, we pulled up outside our little house. We were home. Just the three of us, and then it sunk in …. I was a Mammy.

Brad made us a brew while I walked Nyla around the house talking to her and showing her each room, (because I'm sure she was interested.) We then settled her down for the night in her Moses basket, but no sooner had I got my jammy's on, when she let out an almighty scream… I had a feeling that our Mondays weren't going to be the same again. Eventually, she stopped crying and settled down, but when she did sleep, I didn't, because I'd lay gazing at her, feeling so blessed at this beautiful miracle we'd created.

We only had one day together before Brad had to return to work, I felt anxious about being on my own, I had no choice though, I had to be strong and carry on, especially because I now had a little person relying on me.

I'd tried my hardest to breast feed Nyla, but it was agonising, it didn't help that the health visitor made me feel a complete failure when I told her that I'd decided to switch to formula feeding.

I knew in my heart it wasn't working but my head was telling me different as it usually did. I was finding it hard because Nyla was an unsettled baby, it didn't matter what I tried with her she would scream. Her little legs would raise up to her chest and she cried inconsolably on and off for hours, throughout the day. She'd then at exactly six o'clock, crash out and sleep until six in the morning. If she hadn't, I really don't know how I'd have coped. I felt so helpless because I just wanted to ease her pain. Even after the consultant had prescribed Infacol and Gaviscon for reflux, it didn't make a difference.

I learnt very quickly that I was going to be judged for having a baby that cried all the time, "*Oh, listen to that poor baby*" and "*God what a good set of lungs,*" and this irritated the shit out of me, I tried to ignore the comments, but it was so hard. They picked the wrong day when I stood in the que in marks and Spencer's and I'd had enough, "*Oh, is she hungry,*" "*Maybe she's tired,*" "*Tut, tut.*" I felt like the worst mother in the world, incapable of caring for my own baby, as her cries got louder, and people were staring. I tried to comfort her and ignore the judgmental pricks around me. Inevitably though it all got too much, and I just snapped, dropping my basket to the ground, and yelled, *"If you think you can do a better job, please feel free!"* I walked as fast as I could to the car park and burst into tears and continued to cry all the way home. After hours of rubbing her tummy, laying her in different positions, rocking her, changing her nappy, feeding her, and dancing her around the room to the song *"Would I lie to you,"* (which would strangely stop her sometimes.) I just couldn't take it anymore; I could feel my heart palpitating. I carefully lowered her into the pram, collapsing by the front door with my head in my hands. I then cried for a solid hour.

Why couldn't I cope? Why did I feel this way? I began to avoid family and friends, through both fear and self-consciousness. To ask for help was unthinkable, she was my baby, and she was my responsibility. It felt like every time anyone visited especially the health visitor, she slept as if proving me to be a liar. I was adamant that my baby hated me, I felt she blamed me for the traumatic start I gave her in life. I was physically and emotionally exhausted, I was no longer able to look after myself and every day became too much effort. I felt so sad all the time, reduced to tears at the slightest thing, but what overwhelmed me the most was the guilt I felt that I hadn't bonded with my baby. I would never dream of telling anyone how I felt through that time, they'd be disgusted in me. I felt that I was failing my baby every single day. I was petrified that if I did tell anyone, they'd take her away from me.

When Nyla was four months old, I had to return to work. I felt so apprehensive about the whole situation, how could I leave her when she was so unsettled, it was too soon, but I also couldn't afford to pay my maternity back.

I dropped Nyla off to my Mam before my late shift, running out before they saw me blubbing, my stomach was in knots because I didn't want to leave my baby. I spent most of the shift making excuses to use the toilet to go and cry. I also made the mistake of ringing mam to check in on Nyla, wishing I hadn't as it made me feel ten times worse. In between shifts I was either crying or wanted to sleep, I just didn't feel right.

If I was honest with myself, I hadn't felt right since giving birth. I started having panic attacks, I couldn't breathe and felt suffocated because of these deep dark thoughts and feelings. Surely this wasn't normal, this should be the happiest time of my life.

Nyla had an appointment with the doc one morning when I bumped into Carrie, the health visitor. She asked me if I was ok and I began to cry, she gave me a big hug and came and sat with me. *"I feel so sad sweetheart, you've lost your sparkle."* She read my mind. The Doc was running late for a change, so I sat and told her everything. It wasn't until I sat and talked to her that I realised just how bad I felt. I couldn't keep my emotions hidden any longer. Carrie then came with me to see my doctor. He asked me a series of questions about how I felt, and I had to rate each answer out of ten. He also reassured me that I had nothing to be embarrassed or ashamed of. *"The most important thing is that you've been honest about how you feel and that's the first step to helping yourself."* Carrie also suggested that I have a think about work and that the most important thing right now, was to get myself better. The Doc told me that I was suffering from post-natal depression, he suggested I try medication. After years of counselling and CBT, I agreed to try it. It wasn't just me I had to think of now, I had a family and I had to be well again. I felt so relieved, I just knew immediately that I'd made the right decision. You know that gut instinct that is so often ignored, my advice is listen because that gut instinct is always right.

My doctor then wrote me a prescription for my first antidepressant, along with a sick note to quit my job.

I was relying on these bad boys to change my life. I didn't know then that these were going to be my crutch for the rest of my life. They were my *'crazy pills'*…

It's ok baby, we've got this

Am I always going to feel like this? I asked myself one morning. My body ached with exhaustion, while my mind was drained with emotion. I perched on the edge of the bed, watching my beautiful baby girl sleeping in her crib, knowing that deep in my heart I'd do everything in my power to always love and protect her.

I soon began to realise that it didn't matter what chapter of life I was living, the past always seemed to find a way of reappearing when I least expected. I tried to cope with it as best as I could, but some days were harder than others. My secret inner pain lingered, with those around me completely unaware. I hadn't even told Brad which hurt so bad. I prayed that when I swallowed that first pill, my life would change for the better. I hoped that the dark thoughts and feelings would be erased from my mind for good. I thought of it as a comfort blanket wrapped around me. It made me feel safe and gave me a feeling of warmth and reassurance which I craved.

After a few weeks, my mood had started to lift, and I became a little less tearful. Day by day I started to feel more like my old bubbly self, the more positive I felt, the less stressed I was. I'd found a balance between feeding, cleaning, naps and playtime and could finally appreciate every precious moment with Nyla, which had become a lot easier since she had settled into becoming a happy and playful little girl. She was my little buddy, and we did everything together. We'd play for hours together with the '*Fimbles*' while watching Disney movies on repeat. Nyla continued to prove the consultants wrong with her progress, her strength just amazed me every single day. By the time she was six months old, she was discharged from the hospital, the screaming and crying was replaced with laughter and mischief. Don't get me wrong, we had our difficult days, I just learnt to ride through them. I did begin to question my parenting again when Nyla refused to walk, not because she couldn't, but because she wouldn't. She thought it was much more fun to crawl at a hundred miles an hour than it was to walk, because that was just way too much effort. I'd laugh as she'd turned and grinned at me, with her big blue eyes and her mop of auburn hair.

As Nyla grew, our once cosy little house had started to feel a bit squished. Nyla loved to be outside, but we just didn't have the room for her to play, so we decided to look for a home with more space and a garden.

Someone once told me that moving to a new house can take years off your life, I didn't know what they meant ... well shit the bed, I do now! It wasn't so much the packing and organising either, because I found that was the most exciting part, for me it was the solicitors that caused the most stress. Oh, and the time wasters that I swear purely arranged a viewing for nothing more than a snoop around your home, which I'm sure at least seven out of the nine viewings I had one day fell into that exact category, especially the guy joined by a group of five lads. In a tiny two bed terraced house, seriously? Then there are the ones that feel that need to literally open, shut, poke and prod almost anything and everything and then say they aren't interested, even when I had the scent of coffee brewing in the kitchen, in the hope that it would win someone over.

Coincidentally though after all that when we did sell the house, it was to a friend of a friend, and it all worked out well, so we were really pleased.

In the meantime, we fell in love with a semidetached house situated in a quiet street. Brad and I just knew it was the house for us, with the open hallway, gorgeous bay windows and most importantly a good-sized garden. We couldn't wait to move in.

I was going to miss Rosa so much and our hours of chatting over a brew, (or should I say in the mornings it was a milky coffee at eleven o'clock with a plate of biscuits and if it was in the afternoon, it would be a strong brew in a teapot in a matching cup and saucer.) Every other week we'd walk up to the cemetery together and she would chat away to her lost loved ones, as she laid beautiful carnations and roses and polished their grey shiny headstones. We reassured Rosa that we weren't going far and would only ever be at the other end of the phone if she needed us.

Eventually, we received a letter with our moving date and December 15 the 2006, couldn't come quick enough.

I loved Christmas so much, with this being Nyla's first it was going to be even more special. Despite being knackered on the day of the move, I found myself frantically searching through boxes for the Christmas deccys. I was determined to make this Christmas as magical as I could. Squinting, I looked at the time, it was two am. But the look on Nyla's face the next morning was well worth my tiredness. I poured myself a coffee and prepared myself for another busy day ahead.

Christmas day soon arrived, and it was lovely, we were even able to invite all our family with the extra space we had.

After Christmas I was offered a job in a nursing home Just along the road from us. It was night shifts looking after Alzheimer's and dementia patients. The Nursing home had a nice feel about it, and the patients living in were so sweet. I enjoyed working again but the nights really took a toll on me, I started to be taken advantage of, and soon found myself working five nights a week, with no sleep. The more I did, the more was expected of me, and the pressure became too much. I was tired and mardy, and it wasn't fair on Nyla, so I decided to give it up, besides, she wasn't going to be little forever, and I wanted to make the most out of every minute with her.

Brad and I had always wanted our babies close together, so just after Nyla's first birthday we decided to try for baby number two. I had to make an appointment with my doctor to discuss my medication first and he agreed to gradually reduce my dose of antidepressants. I was worried about my mental health but hoped the excitement of the future would distract me. I assumed it was going to be as easy as the first time around, as I threw away my last pill packet. However, one month, after another month, after another, I started to worry that something was wrong. Desperate to find out why I couldn't conceive, we made an appointment at the surgery.

"What's the appointment for?" the receptionist rudely asked Brad, while I legged it around the waiting room chasing Nyla. *"Erm, it's to find out why she can't fall pregnant, a sperm test I think"*, I heard him answer, my face burning with embarrassment. I literally wanted the ground to swallow me up. The line behind us was getting longer and all eyes were on me, as I attempted to detain my crazy toddler. Oh, I knew exactly what they were thinking. We didn't have much luck with the doctor either, so we decided to make an appointment for a consultation at a private hospital, hopeful for answers. The consultant was efficient and

thorough as well as expensive. After various tests and scans, I was diagnosed with polycystic ovaries, which made my chances slimmer of falling pregnant. I felt like it had become an impossible dream to give Nyla a brother or sister and I felt guilty that I felt this way, I should have been thankful that I had a healthy little one already, and of course I was, but the more your heart desires something the stronger the determination is, and failure isn't an option.

After a few months we decided to take the pressure of ourselves, from using ovulation tests to doing handstands on the bed (yep, we tried everything) by accepting that everything happens for a reason and maybe it wasn't meant to be.

I tried to put it to the back of my mind, and I returned to work at the hospital. I had missed nursing so much, so I joined the bank staff as it gave me the flexibility to work my hours around our little family.

I worked a couple of night shifts a week around the hospital, but I somehow always found myself back on the Gynaecology ward. "*Sorry, me again*", I'd smile as I walked onto the ward.

"*How about working here permanently three nights a week?*", the ward sister asked me one shift. Smiling I didn't even need to think about it and said yes right away. The hours suited us perfectly and Mam kindly offered to help with Nyla, so I could get a couple of hours of sleep after my shift, but I tended to spend most of the time cleaning the house and ringing her to make sure Nyla was ok, catching an hour's kip if I was lucky. Not that it really bothered me because I'd finally found another job that I loved and felt happy in. The hardest part for me was the heartache of the angel babies. There are no words and no matter how hard I tried I couldn't change my own sensitive nature, I felt so deeply for their losses and even though I behaved in a professional manner, the tears would come later on my way home. That was just me, it always had been, and I guess it always will be.

A few months later I had started to feel exhausted and low, I just put it down to working night shifts, lack of sleep and chasing after a toddler so I carried on regardless, well that was until my period was late ….

Four positive pregnancy tests later, no… five just to be sure like. I couldn't contain my excitement, wanting to share my news with the world knowing I had to be patient. Right from the start this pregnancy was completely different to my first. I craved the most random foods like piccalilli. As the pregnancy continued my health started to suffer and I ended up in and out of hospital. I didn't want to give up my job, but I also knew that I was struggling, and I had to put myself and my baby first. My heart ached for the patients that had lost their babies so much that I tried hard to disguise my own growing bump. I know pregnancy happens all the time, but I just felt it was insensitive because they dealt with such grief. It was also enhancing my own anxieties as I knew from the environment in which I was working in what actually could go wrong. I had a chat with the ward sister about how I felt, she completely understood, and she encouraged me to return after the birth of my baby.

I knew I'd made the right decision to leave when I did because soon after I was admitted to hospital several times with complications. I had a reoccurring kidney infection which resulted in me having to take antibiotics for the remainder of the pregnancy. I'd perch on the edge of the sofa with a heat bag on my back for sciatica, support belt around my bump with my legs wide open and yoghurt on my vag, due to the constant thrush I now had to deal with. (Apologies if I have just put you off your dinner) I was then admitted to hospital at twenty weeks as they suspected I was going into premature labour, I felt petrified as I lay there as the midwifes and doctors monitored my baby. Thankfully, it was a false alarm and they advised me to rest up.

I worried throughout the pregnancy, especially when my consultant encouraged me to try for a natural birth after the traumatic experience with Nyla. I expressed my concerns and he agreed that if my baby hadn't arrived by the due date, they would then book me in for an elective c section on the 6 th of march. Hoping my baby had heard the conversation and would patiently wait until that date, and as if by a miracle my due date passed, and I was admitted into hospital on the 6 th of March 2009....

Experiencing an elective c-section was a completely different experience altogether, the atmosphere was calm and relaxed, there was music playing on a radio and within twenty minutes I had this beautiful baby boy, placed on my chest. My heart was filled with love, tears of joy rolled down my cheeks and every pain and every worry had vanished. I looked up at Brad smiling.

"Billy?" He asked.

"Definitely," I nodded. I felt completely overwhelmed and thankful that my precious baby boy had been delivered safely.

The midwife on the ward was obviously aware by my notes that this was my second birth, as she poked her head round the curtain and muttered, *"c'mon you know what you're doing, you've done it before".* She couldn't have been more wrong. The truth was I had absolutely no idea what I was doing at all. I felt so lost as I looked down at my new baby's little scrunched up face and I whispered to him,

"It's ok baby, we've got this".

So, with the curtains drawn around us I just taught myself how to feed my baby, and I felt proud. I didn't need anyone else. I just wished the woman opposite would get the hell off her phone, it had been glued to her ear most of the time, mind you she soon got her comeuppance as I had the most painful trapped wind ever and farted continually that night.

Billy was such a content baby, Nyla absolutely adored him, my heart would melt as

I watched Nyla's once tiny hand hold onto his. I couldn't believe how big she looked now.

We felt content and complete in our little family, and we couldn't wait to create special memories with them.

I hadn't decided if, or when I was going to return to work yet as much as we needed the money, spending time with my babies meant more to me.

Every day the three of us would go for a long walk, Billy would be in his pram with his taggy and binky, Nyla would run ahead in her Peppa pig wellies splashing in every single puddle, well that was until she complained that her legs were tired, and she needed a pram too. I compromised by letting her sit on the end of the pram, so she was happy, not sure Billy was best pleased, but he was smiling.

I would take them to playgroups which I absolutely hated. I found them to be so judgemental so I would often take them to the library instead, let's face it books didn't give you dirty looks, well most of them didn't anyway.

As Family life became a routine of chores and caring for my little people all day, every day with Brad most often working, boxing or playing cricket at the weekends, I began to feel lonely and being at home with my babies all the time got me thinking. This wasn't always a good thing for me, so I did what I did best and began to worry. A lot.

I started suffering with heart palpitations, I'd panic that I had upset someone, or I had done something wrong, it seems so trivial now but to me it was a big deal. I'd bite my nails until they bled, it felt like I had scraped through and now the darkness was back yet again to destroy any chance of happiness. I cared so deeply for everyone else, the last thing I wanted to do was burden anyone with my troubles, so I just smiled and carried on regardless.

I knew deep down 'it' was back with a vengeance, only this time that cloud was even darker than before, and I didn't know which way to turn. As I stood in the hallway rocking Billy back and forth to sleep in his pram, I noticed a small mark on the corner of the mirror in the lounge, it had to be cleaned now, it couldn't wait, how could I have missed it, I felt my entire body tense up, I fell to the floor and broke down shaking uncontrollably, unable to breathe I tried to calm myself down. The strong emotions of anger, frustration and great sadness washed over me so heavily that I felt physically ill.

I was trying so hard to keep it together for my babies, I wanted to protect them as much as I possibly could. The last thing I wanted was for any of this to affect their childhood, so I just had to try to be the best mum that I could, and to do that I had to be honest with myself, I had to admit that I needed help.

I closed my eyes, took a breath and stood up wiping away my tears. I could feel the heat across my chest as it spread up my neck, leaving behind a blotchy red rash, trying not to scratch it as I normally did, I found a pen in the kitchen a wrote myself a note and put it next to the kettle.

'Ring Doc'

I found myself once again, with my leg shaking, sitting on that plastic red chair in the waiting room of the surgery.

The doctor was staring at the computer screen as I walked in, '*Yes*', *he* said abruptly.

I told him how I felt, and without hesitation he wrote a prescription for the previous medication I had taken.

'*Give it four weeks, then make another appointment*', he said, passing me the piece of paper.

I'd taught myself to bury my feelings deep for so long that it had become natural. I had to accept that the abuse was in the past, but in order for me to survive I had to swallow a pill to keep it there.

Hold on tight, here we go again, back on that rollercoaster.

Warriors never give up

Once again, I picked myself up, brushed myself down and I started all over again. I began to once again knock back high doses of psychiatric drugs on a repeat prescription. I was doing ok…for now.

It was early one Saturday morning when I woke up to a strange text message of Mam.

"Ring me when you're up." I felt that sick feeling you get at the pit of my stomach when you just know something isn't right. My heart thudded as I called her.

Immediately I heard the worry in her voice, *"Your Dad's been rushed into hospital with a suspected stroke."* They were away at their second home at the time, which was a two-hour drive away. I had to be with them and even though I'd never driven that distance before, but without hesitation I grabbed my keys and left the house.

It's a journey that I'll never forget and whenever I doubt myself, I will always think back to that moment and remind myself that I can in fact do anything.

The roads were the clearest that I'd ever see them, almost like it had been paved just for me, as unbelievable as that may sound.

Mam was sat in her dressing gown in shock, a cold brew sat on table next to her. I stomach churned on the thirty-minute drive to the hospital to see Dad, having no idea what to expect once there. I walked on to the ward and saw him sitting looking all bewildered wearing as what I can only describe as a bright orange convict's overall, as if he was awaiting a jail sentence, which I obviously joked about, not knowing how I was to react to the whole situation. I burst into tears and gave him the biggest hug I could squeeze out.

Dad was so confused bless him and although I tried to talk to him, he couldn't understand what I was saying. I could see the frustration in his face and the fear in his eyes as he didn't know what was happening to him.

I stayed as late as I could before reluctantly having to say goodbye to them both. I didn't want to leave him there and I wanted to bring him home, but at the same time I was worried about Nyla and Billy. I drove Mam back and settled her in and then headed for home. To be honest I can't really remember much about the journey home because my mind was a complete blur with worry about the both of them being so far away and how helpless I felt.

I pulled up outside our house and gathered my thoughts for a few minutes before I went in. I had just poured myself a brew when my phone rang. *'Oh shit'* I thought, I'd forgot to give Mam three rings to let her know I was home safe.

"Dads had another stroke!" she sobbed *"This time it's worse."* she paused.
"He's completely lost his speech and he can't communicate at all."
I fell to the floor. I had to be there for them. I knew they needed my support now more than

ever and it was now my turn to look after them.

I couldn't settle so at 3am, careful not to wake everyone I went up into the loft and brought down the suitcases and packed one each for me, Nyla and Billy.

As soon as they woke up, I told them that we were going on a *'wee road trip'* and that Grampy was very poorly, he needed us to help look after him. Nyla was happy at the fact she didn't have to go to nursery whereas Billy had no idea what was going on, other than the fact he knew it was time for his morning Weetabix lobbing session.

My thoughts were racing, I just couldn't comprehend the fact that Dad couldn't communicate, he was the most outgoing person I knew. He loved nothing more than having a laugh and a chat. It's what we all knew and loved about him.

It wasn't the easiest of journeys with a three and one year old, but we made it and I know I am biased, but I can honestly say that they were just amazing. Their understanding and behaviour with everything going on around them, I couldn't have felt prouder of them.

I knew I had to be strong and stay calm and I've always brought my children up with honesty, and that's exactly how I handled this situation. I explained to them that Grampy had suffered with a bleed on the brain called a stroke and it was our job to look after him. They just accepted it in their stride bless them and we took each day as it came.

"Hi Dad" I smiled.

His face appeared drooped slightly to one side and he looked exhausted. He couldn't communicate at all. I tried to stay positive, but the consultant said it was early days, so we didn't have many answers.

We stayed with Mam and would visit Dad twice a day at the hospital, which was a forty-five-minute drive away. In between visiting Dad I'd be on the phone to concerned family and friends, and as draining as it was for me it was even harder for Mam. Her world had been completely turned upside down, and she was doing all she could to hold it together.

We passed on the daily well wishes to Dad, but he was adamant he wanted no visitors he would shake his head and get himself in a state if anyone asked to visit. It just wasn't him at all, he loved to be around people. We knew it was going to be a challenge to express his wishes to family and friends, but they also needed to understand that they were to be respected. I'm sure deep down the reason for his decision was mostly down to embarrassment, he couldn't even ask to use the toilet bless his heart. We tried to communicate with him through writing and drawing but he couldn't understand which then made it more frustrating for him.

My heart broke for him, especially when he was trying so hard to get his words out. He looked so vulnerable, and I felt so helpless.

The doctors told us that it'd be months until we knew if he'd make any kind of recovery. He couldn't read, he couldn't write, and the stroke had affected his eyes so badly that he could no longer drive.

Driving was Dad's life and I worried how much this was all going to impact on his life, especially with him being such a proud man.

Despite my dad's wishes, the one person to completely ignore them was Nathan, who insisted on visiting.

For some reason Nathan was full of resentment towards me. I felt sick, and I felt angry but as always, I had no choice in the matter so I suggested to Mam that she meet him at the hospital, and I would take the chance to have some quiet time with Nyla and Billy.

I was so pissed when late that evening, they turned up. I had literally just settled the children to sleep. I immediately felt the atmosphere change and made my excuses to go to bed. Not only was I trying to come to terms with all this, but I now had all this hurt brewing up inside of me that I really didn't need to deal with right now.

The next morning, we arrived at the hospital just in time for the Doctor's rounds. We couldn't believe it when he told us that Dad was going to be discharged. We assumed he meant to a closer hospital to where we lived until he said the word *'home'*. Wait what does he mean home??! Are you actually kidding me? I asked Mam. My head went into overdrive with questions, but my mouth wouldn't move to ask them. How the hell were they going to cope? What if he has another stroke? Of course, we wanted nothing more than for Dad to be in the comfort of his own home. Surely this was too soon though, there was no support or advice given he was literally discharged as if leaving with his leg in a plaster cast.

I felt so scared for him especially with the way the stroke had occurred, it wasn't like you see on the advert either. He came over all confused and disoriented, it was difficult to tell immediately what was happening to him which I think was even more frightening.

We knew that we had a challenging road ahead of us, but we had to remain strong and positive for Dad. He had always been the breadwinner, the head of the family. Mam suffered with agoraphobia, so Dad had always taken on the responsibilities from driving to finances. Suddenly all of that had been taken away from him, and their roles had been completely reversed. Mam's life was going to change dramatically, starting with the two-hour drive home from the hospital, which she had never done before. I praised her as much as I could without patronising, as I knew how hard she was finding it all.

Gradually the more she did, her confidence grew enough to take on the tasks that she knew she had to do, like the weekly hospital appointments. I did all I could to support them when I could and often Brad would come in the door as I'd be going out.

With time and a lot of patience Dad was able to say odd words, which then led into a couple of sentences. Unfortunately, his reading, writing and numbers didn't return and never fully would and yet all the time he would try his best to deal with life with humour as he always did, and I swear that's what got him through. It was his strength. Dad being Dad was just so grateful to be alive. He had proved to the world what a real warrior was, and he had taught me that when the going gets tough, you never give up.

I'd well up when Nyla and Billy jumped on Grampy's knee with a story book, eager for him to read it, he would just stare blankly at the pages until Nyla would say *"Don't worry Grampy, I'll read it to you as I'm a big girl now".* She would then go on to read the story pronouncing all the letters and words so Grampy could understand, bless her.

Sadly, over the years I've had to sadly watch many of my much loved hard-working family and friends who have never been able to take a break or slow down, even when their body is telling them to take it easy. But due to the demands and pressures of life they feel that they can't, that is until that decision is taken away from them and the lesson learnt is too late. This made me realise that you really do need to '*cherish yesterday, dream of tomorrow and live for today.*' Because life is too short to do anything but that.

Meanwhile, I didn't realise just how much the resentment with Nathan was building up, well that was until he barged his way into my home demanding to know why I was helping so much. I had no idea what his problem was and thought I should maybe take a step back in case everyone else felt the same. I just always went with my heart and maybe I'd gone too far. Either way he left me questioning myself when he tried to stir trouble by suggesting that Hollie also felt the same. He was slowly trying to turn the whole family against me. I couldn't believe he had the audacity to stand there in my hallway looking at me in a way that will never leave me. I fought back the tears as I firmly told him he was wrong and that I never meant to upset anyone, that I would now back off and let him take over if that's how he felt.

In that moment, as he walked out of my front door something had changed inside me and I knew that I didn't have to keep feeling frightened like this, I wasn't that little girl anymore.

I started to question myself, and my life. Whatever it all meant, I knew that after he had left things were never going to be the same again. I was fed up with being spoken to like shit and I refused to let him speak to me like that ever again.

I did broach the subject with Mam, and I told her I thought it was best that I backed off because it was causing too much upset, but she disagreed. I told her that she only ever had to tell me if she did feel that way even though she continued to insist she didn't. I hated to think I was upsetting others I just always thought with my heart not my head that's just how I was.

The pressure and the shit stirring had all got too much and Hollie and I ended up having a fight over it all. We rarely fell out and it was breaking me not being able to talk to her. One thing that had been playing on my mind a lot and it was beginning to trouble me deeply was one of the last things she said to me.

"I've kept something to myself for years, no one knows anything about" she screamed at me. *'Oh my god, oh shit, please no!'* I prayed she'd not gone through what I had.

I couldn't stop thinking about what Hollie had said. The memories of my abuse surfaced once again, only this time something felt different, I had stomach pains and I felt sick with dread. I knew that I couldn't go on until I had spoken to Hollie, but before I did, I had to find the courage to tell Brad *everything*.

This was going to be the hardest thing I'd ever had to do. I knew that once I'd spoken the truth that there was no turning back. So, after seventeen years I was ready to talk. I had to be strong, and I had to do it
NOW.
The biggest fear that I felt was that I wasn't going to be believed.

An ocean of secrets

There are two types of secrets, the one you make as a promise the other is the kind you don't ever dare tell through fear.

I checked in on Nyla and Billy as they lay peacefully sleeping, whispering *'love you always'* then as I crept out. I then took a deep breath as I walked into our bedroom.

Brad was sitting on the bed as I searched for the words to say, quietly I whispered, *"There's something I need to tell you."*

Looking up, I think he knew it was serious, *"What's up?"* he asked

"It's something that happened to me when I was little." I told him.

He started to look concerned as he put his phone down on the bedside table. Painfully and emotionally I then had to revisit my past and pray he listened, although I never expected him to understand.

As I began, *"I was seven and a half..."*
The words continued to flow, almost as if something had awakened within me having no intention of supressing itself any longer.

I closed my eyes and took myself back to that painful time in my life and continued to tell Brad my *secret*.

I can still see myself sitting there in the middle room of the house playing on the red carpet. I would do this thing when I was young that when I was engrossed with something, I would jump on my knees as I got a little carried away as my Sylvanians bear family were going on a vacation on their blue canal boat. I loved playing with those little animal families dressed in their frilly little dresses and dungarees.

That was when it happened. The first time. I remember having that feeling you get when you think someone else is there with you, I looked up and saw Nathan standing in the doorway, he was watching me play. He then told me to go with him into the toilet and he sexually abused me.

I always knew what was coming and as I got older, I would pretend to be having my period to avoid it knowing he would soon see past that excuse.

What scared me the most was that he let nothing stop him, not even my Mam being in the house, and as Mam's do, she would be busy with her chores and he always seemed to know when she was distracted, so I soon realised that I didn't have safe place anymore.

Taking a moment, I paused and looked over at Brad who was just sat there in silence, staring straight ahead.

I was struggling to read his reaction, I think it must have been shock and I needed to give him time, I couldn't even begin to imagine how I would have felt or reacted had it have been the reverse.

I had thought that his immediate reaction would have been to deck Nathan, but instead he became quiet and withdrew into himself, it was as though he could feel my pain and was powerless to do anything about it.

Over the years Brad had always questioned why I had read so many autobiographical books written by abuse victims I think it then suddenly dawned on him.

"Fuck, it's because you relate to them."

I nodded with tears running down my cheeks.

He was right, I had read so many accounts by innocent victims, most of whom like me had felt too frightened to confide anyone.

I think he must have questioned why I had never said anything before and why now even. I had told him that Hollie had made a comment and I was worried that she had gone through the same. I needed to put my mind at rest by asking her. I knew it was time for the truth to come out, it had weighed me down for too long. I just prayed that by me not saying anything it hadn't caused anyone else suffering.

I felt nervous as I walked across the road to my sister's house and although it was a little awkward at first, I guess it always is after you've had a disagreement with someone, we went into the front room, and we sat down. I hesitated for a minute and then said, *"Ok I'm just going to come out with this now."*

Hollie was looking over at me with a blank expression.

"Please tell me it didn't happen to you as well, please."

It was clear by her reaction that she was confused, I knew that I was going to have to ask her outright if our brother had ever sexually abused her. Then I realised that, that's exactly what it was what had happened to me, sexual abuse. I could tell she was in complete shock.

"I feel so bad as I only said that in heat of the moment, no he never touched me!"

Her emotions then turned to anger as she started shouting, *"The bastard!"* *"How could he do this to you?"*. *"Why didn't you tell me or anyone, I'm your sister we tell each other everything."*

I'd never see my sister like this before, I was the one that was always swearing not her. I knew she was right, but I just wanted to protect her. I could tell she was angry with herself for not suspecting a thing, which made me feel so bad because I didn't want to shift any blame onto her, especially guilt because none of this was her fault.

While I was relieved that she was ok and hadn't had to endure the same pain that I had, it had also unleashed overwhelming emotions in me for the first time and I broke down, she sat beside me and held my hand to comfort me.

I had opened up an ocean full of secrets and I was petrified of the consequences it may have.

I didn't want to cause any trouble in the family, the last thing I wanted was to upset anyone, so I begged Hollie not to tell a soul. I knew for certain I didn't want Mam and Dad to know as it would destroy them.

Dad had remained very fragile after having his strokes, I didn't want to be the cause of another.

Before I left, we cried and we hugged, and I left with any bad feelings forgotten and felt nothing but love and support from her.

Behind the façade of a fake smile and brave face, which I had now mastered to perfection, all this had now unnerved me, and I didn't know what to do with it.

You know that feeling you get in your tummy when you're a child when either you or a sibling has broken something and your scared shitless that one of them will tell tales and you would be in trouble. I always wondered if all of this had affected Nathan in that way. He did the naughty thing, and I could have told at any time, but I didn't.

Had he lived forever looking over his shoulder in fear that he would get found out? Then again perhaps he didn't.

Maybe he always knew he would get away with it because of his controlling and manipulative behaviour. He was so sure of himself and had got away with it for so long all he had to do was deny it anyway. The main thing was he felt safe, leaving me feeling the complete opposite.

It didn't matter how much I tried to push the thoughts away they just wouldn't budge. I was worried that if I contacted social services, they wouldn't take me seriously and I didn't want them to think I was wasting their time, but I also had to do whatever I could to protect others.

As much as I had tried to hide it from my Mam, it all just came out one day and all I can believe is that, it did for reason. Mam and I were chatting away in the car as we did when we went shopping. The conversation went from life to kids, to unexpectedly a subject about

Nathan that just provoked me. Completely catching me off guard and without thinking I just blurted it out, in fact more like I screamed it out in frustration.

It was too late.

I couldn't shuv what I had just disclosed back into my mouth, all I could feel was numb. I don't think I will ever be able to describe how I felt afterwards. I didn't dare look at her.

We sat there, in the car park in complete silence. She must have felt so overwhelmed.

My poor Mam. What had I done? What was she meant to think or feel?

Two of her children who she had nurtured all their lives had kept an unspeakable secret. I couldn't imagine how she felt. I cried and cried as I pleaded with her not to tell my dad, I couldn't bear him finding out about it. I remember repeating myself over and over,

"Have I done the right thing? Have I? please tell me? Shouldn't I have said anything?"

I was desperately seeking reassurance, but she remained silent and looked really upset. I had to understand that this was not going to be easy for her either. The last thing I said on the matter was that I was going to be contacting someone, because I was struggling to cope with it all being brought back up.

I walked through my front door feeling sick to my stomach and the guiltiest I'd ever felt in my life, it sure wasn't quite the sense of relief I'd thought it would be.

It had been a proper shit week and I was getting flashbacks daily. I was irritable with my family and it wasn't fair for me to take my hurt out on them. I took my phone from my bag and typed in the search bar *NSPCC*. I jotted down the contact number and called them.

Then the shit hit the fan

"Hello, you're through to the NSPCC helpline, sorry for the wait how can I help you?"

I sighed with relief when I heard a friendly female voice. Rather than blurting it out or rambling on like I normally did, I contemplated each and every word as they slowly left my mouth.

"Hi there, I'm sorry to bother you, but..." I began.

"The thing is I'm not in a good place. I was abused when I was younger and I'm struggling to cope with life right now."

The lady on end of the line remained calm and supportive throughout the conversation as she carefully repeated what I had just told her. She then reassured me that I'd done the right thing by contacting them before praising me for my

bravery. *"No matter how long-ago, abuse is abuse."*
I didn't feel brave though, I just felt pure guilt
and shame at what I'd just done. As reassuring
as her words may have been, it didn't stop me
from rushing to the bathroom to throw up.
What the fuck had I done now.

After hanging up a sense of dread
washed over me, and I felt scared. I began to
shake knowing that everyone was going to find
out about my shameful secret. I then continued
to pace the house for another half an hour
when my mobile rang with a withheld phone
number.

*"Hi there, my name is Jan. I'm not sure if you were
expecting me to contact you, I'm an investigating police
officer.*
*I'm just calling regarding a historical abuse case that's
been reported to us."*

Wait, what? I assumed that must have been what they called it, *'historical abuse'*, God it even had a name.

It hurt like hell when she asked me to repeat it all again, so I just told her briefly what had happened, choking on my tears. The more that I began to talk the increased pain I felt at the memories that were coming back.

The police officer went on to inform me that I had an important decision to make, but I had no idea what she was talking about. *"You now need to decide whether or not you're going to report the abuse officially and although I can't influence that decision, I strongly advise that you do because it's a serious matter."* I was in too much shock to take this in. *"But what would happen?"* I asked quietly.

"He would be arrested immediately and then be taken to the police station for questioning." She said firmly.

Instinctively, I knew that I couldn't do that to my family. I couldn't expect them to choose sides either. I then imagined his face and for the first time in a long time, I felt sorry for him. I wasn't interviewed officially about my case because I chose not to take it any further. At the end of the day, it's my word against his. How could I ever prove that at seven years old he did what he did? What evidence did I have? All I had was a lifetime of damage and mental health issues which would mean nothing in court. All it would prove is his manipulative behaviour, my words being twisted and turned in every which way they possibly could. No, I just didn't have the strength or the energy for that.

A couple of weeks later I received a phone call suggesting counselling may be the way forward to help me come to terms with everything, but the truth was I didn't give a shit about myself enough to do anything anymore.

I began to doubt everything, convincing myself I'd made it up in my head or I was just being my usual over sensitive self and making a mountain out of a mole hill. Besides this was nothing compared to what others must go through in life.

However, it didn't matter how much I tried to bury my head, the guilt and shame continued to chip away at me. I didn't know how to cope with my emotions now that I couldn't hide from them. I'd stupidly removed my protective blanket that had been wrapped so tightly around me for so long, leaving me feeling vulnerable and unsafe. I was once again that frightened little girl.

I repeatedly asked myself, how could I just put a close to this chapter of my life? Would I ever be able to move on? How can I help myself?

It then became clear to me that there was something that I could do, and it was going to take all the strength and courage I had within me.

I needed to face my fears and confront this situation head on. God this was going to be so hard. The only way I felt that I could express myself was through writing, so I made the decision to write him a letter.

I began to write, but in despair I ripped it up twice. I then stood up and went outside into the garden and breathed in the fresh air before returning to the dining table.

Closing my eyes for a minute, I took a deep breath, put my pen to the blank white sheet of paper and began to let my words flow naturally.

It was written. It was finished and now all I had to do was to find the nerve to send it.

It was early on a Saturday morning that I decided to hand deliver the letter on the way to my hairdressers' appointment. Hoping that it was too early for them to see me, I parked at the top of the street where he lived. After a few minutes of doubting myself again and overthinking that it was a bad idea, I put my seat belt back on and went to turn the key in the ignition. I then stopped. I turned off the engine and picked up the letter. My hands were shaking like a leaf as I slowly walked down the street. Gently, I opened the gate leading up the path to the front door, careful not to make a sound on the crunchy gravel, I pushed the letter through the letterbox, and I ran back to the car as quick as I could and drove off. I'd done it.

For the first time in my life, I'd stood up to someone. Someone I'd looked up to had stolen my entire being and I wasn't prepared to let him take away my future.

I fidgeted about swivelling on the squeaky salon chair, staring ahead watching my hairdresser's lips moving in the mirror, while my mind was on over drive with the words of my letter spinning round in my head…

"I'm not quite sure how to start this letter because I never imagined I'd have to write it.

I think you know what I am referring to and as a young girl I was naïve, and I was vulnerable. But not anymore.

I'm now an adult trying to make sense of what happened at the same time as trying to find the strength to cope with what you did to me. You took away my innocence without a second thought and you made me believe it was normal.

I've never spoken of this until now, but the pain I've had to live with has become so unbearable and has affected every aspect of my life, robbing me of not just my childhood but also my adulthood.

Sadly, I've never felt contentment and probably never will because all I feel is emptiness.

You will be relieved to know, that purely for the sake of the family I won't be taking this further as unfortunately I can't undo what has happened, but I've had to do this to enable myself to release the past and try to move forward as best as I can, if at all possible, that is. Not that I need to explain myself to you.

Please don't take any of this out on any other family members either, they are blameless and that's how it stays.

I really don't know if you've just put this to the back on your mind and moved on, I need you to know that I never have.

Finally, I have written this

with all the pain and hurt you

have left me with. And it stops

here and now."

Stepping out of the salon I could smell the sweetness of the products she'd used on my hair as it blew across my face in the wind (why is it that the weather always knows how to behave when you have literally just had your hair done… the same reason as it does on the school run, I guess!)

I was greeted to the beautiful sound of chaos as I walked into what I called home. The house was a complete carnage, not that I minded as cleaning was my therapy, I would just turn up my tunes and get lost in it.

I set about cleaning and tidying up then I began to prepare Nyla and Billy's lunch when the doorbell rang, licking the butter off my fingers I looked through the blinds. I was always anxious if anyone just turned up without giving me notice. This time I had every reason to feel anxious, because it was Nathan.

I started to shake. Why had he come to my house? This is my safe place.

I looked down at my babies who were obliviously playing together on the rug. I knew I had to answer the door. I had to be strong. I slowly approached the hallway and felt my heart racing as I reached for the door handle.

I had ran and hid too much in the past, it's time to confront this now I told myself as my clammy hands turned the key in the lock. There he stood, as bold as brass.

The man who had destroyed my childhood and taken away my innocence.

He was angry. So angry. *"What's this letter all about then?"* he snapped with a nasty tone in his voice. He comes closer and though I felt intimated by him I tried not to show it as I calmly say to him, *"You know."*

"Nope I have no idea what you're going on about." He snapped again.

I saw red, as it took all my strength not to burst into tears and show even the slightest bit of weakness and managed to find my voice, *"You did that to me, you know you did, please go now."*

As he turns to walk away, he glances back over his shoulder at me and smirked, *"There's nothing you can do about it anyway because you can't prove a thing."* He had his final word.

I slammed the door shut full of anger and hurt.

"No, you bastard I can't." I cried in a heap at the door.

Panic then rises within me because I have a feeling he'll go to Mam and Dad's to cause trouble. Dad especially wouldn't cope with all this. I ring Mam to prepare her, but it was too late. He was already there.

What have I fucking done? Why couldn't I have just kept my big trap shut?

I needed to feel safe, but Brad was playing football and I'd never normally ring him when he was out, so I doubted he'd answer the phone if I called but tried any way and thankfully, he did.

"*What's up?*" he asked in his usual laid-back self.

"*He's been, he's been here*", I cry as I told him what had happened.

"*I'll be fine now I've spoken to you, I just needed to hear your voice because I was scared.*"

Brad wouldn't take no for an answer though and told me to go pick him up.

"*I'm so sorry, I feel so guilty about this*" I apologise to him for the twentieth time as he jumps into the passenger seat of our truck.

I beg him not to cause any trouble (wait, I'm telling *him* not to cause any trouble).

He promises me he won't and asks me to just give him ten minutes to check that Mam and Dad are okay and ask him to leave as they don't need the stress, to which I completely agreed.

As we pull up at the house Nathan's car is parked on the drive.

"Please be careful." I say as Brad shuts the car door. I drove around the block and parked up and waited for what felt like the longest ten minutes of my life.

When I approached the house Nathan passed me in his car and I can tell he's angry as he's gesturing his fist at me in a threatening manner through his car window.

I felt awful. This was all my doing; how could I be so selfish for wanting to move on with my life?

"What's happened?" my accusation must have pissed Brad right off because all he was doing was protecting me so to calm the atmosphere

Dad, as always put the kettle on and we all had a brew not wanting to draw any more attention to what had happened I completely changed the subject, and we didn't speak of it again.

At least I knew I was safe now Brad was at home with me, and we tried to get on with the rest of the day without any more upset.

I had just sat down when my mobile rang, I really couldn't be arsed with talking to anyone but saw it was Mam, so I answered, instead what she told me left me speechless.

"Erm I've just had a visit. From the police, they are on their way to you they need to talk to you and Brad"

"Wait, what are you okay? What's happened?" I asked concerned.

"Nathan's gone to hospital with head injuries, and he's told them that Brad assaulted him."

I couldn't believe it. This was not happening. *He's* the victim?

Sure enough, within five minutes I'm answering my door to two police officers. I was in complete shock as neither of us had ever had any issues with the police and now I'm showing them into my lounge to be questioned. They told us that they had come to inform us of an allegation that had been made against Brad, accusing him of assault and because it was a family matter it would be dealt with as domestic incident, suggesting that with a simple apology it should resolve the matter.

"An apology? Are you kidding me? HE is demanding an apology?" I cried at them.

What really pissed me off is that the officer indicated that Brad was guilty because of his defensive body language. Brad always looked defensive that's just how he was, how dare they question him taking Nathan's side! Brad sat looking straight ahead with his arms folded, continuing to deny the accusation. I just sat there silently wishing that he had kicked the shit out of him now because he didn't deserve any of this. Reminding Brad of his gun licence the officers gave him absolutely no choice but to apologise.

I was shocked at the lengths that he'd gone to, but then I guess he was avoiding any attention on himself.

The officer explained that once his apology had been accepted, we would be able to move on without any hassle.

"Move on?" I sobbed. *"The years I've suffered because of him, he's the one in the wrong, I can't believe that he's doing this to us"*

The officer interrupted me with the fact that they weren't there to talk about the past and I would need to report that officially and it be dealt with at another time.

Dealt with. Yeah right.

Everything around me as falling apart. I felt utterly helpless.

After they had left, I went and ran myself a bath. My head felt like it was going to explode. I had a soak, got into my pjs and just calmed down when my phone rang. It was the police again.

"I'm sorry to inform you but we're going to have to take the matter further as the victim hasn't accepted the apology." He explained to us that they had spent over two hours trying to persuade Nathan to accept the apology, but he was point blank refusing. *"What the actual fuck?"*

The only person responsible for his injuries was himself.

However, after that we heard absolutely nothing from them so we just had this hanging over us, when they eventually did contact us it was to apologise for how busy they were, so surely, they couldn't have taken it that seriously.

The week had gone from bad to worse, especially when my friends were telling me that Nathan's family had been blasting Brad all over social media referring to him as a beast. They continued to create the most farfetched bullshit they possibly could for a reaction, to which they got no response. It was sheer hell, but we knew the truth and we also knew that we had absolutely nothing to hide.

One evening I lit the fire and tackled the mountain of ironing that had piled up with my name on it, when the house phone rang, (which was rare as we had mobile phones) when I answered it was quiet on the other end

"Hello, don't hang up"

Oh god it was *him,* how did he find our number? We were ex-directory for a reason.

"Can I come to the house?" he had the absolute neck of a giraffe this man.

"No way, Brad said you're not welcome, you have to stay away from us."

I won't ever forget the words he said next, mainly because in my mind I know he was admitting what he had done.

"I want to apologise. I still don't know what you're going on about as I can't remember any of it, but I apologise, I suggest you live your life now and I will live mine"

I mumbled and hung up. And then I felt numb.

I went from feeling sorry for him to feeling nothing but anger and hatred towards him.

The truth was that he knew what happened all of them years ago, he hadn't forgotten.

It would take all my strength just to get up in the mornings, I was oblivious to the fact that I had two little people who needed me. I was supressing my emotions daily as I became addicted to drink and prescription drugs to blot out the pain and my life began to once again spiral out of control. I would shout at myself, smack myself around the face and punch myself in frustration. I was sick of living and if something didn't change soon there was only going to be one way out for me. That was until one morning I got up and convinced myself that, *'Today is going to be different.'* I knew that I had to find a way through this pain somehow, not just for my own sake but also my family's.

At that time, I did regret saying something because I believed that by doing so, it had achieved nothing but added pain and hurt to everyone around me. But I couldn't take it back, so I just had to accept it and move forward with my life. He would have to live with what he had done even though I don't think he'll ever feel the pain that I did.

I started therapy and life became settled at home as we moved forward as a family. We were now stronger than ever; my babies and Brad were all that mattered to me now.

I felt even more blessed when we found out we were expecting our third baby. This was the start of a new beginning for us because I knew deep down that our new baby had been sent to us for a reason.

Cause' fixers never fix themselves

Would you like to know the sex of your baby?"
asked the sonographer. We wanted a surprise
with both Nyla and Billy, but as this was going
to be our last baby, we thought it would be
easier if we knew so we could plan.

"You're having a little … girl." I had my heart set
on a beautiful pram, it was navy and white
striped with a red bow and a buggy and car
seat to match. It was perfect. My best friends
Kerry and Lily had arranged a baby shower for
me, putting together the most beautiful basket
full of gifts for our baby girl, bless their hearts.
I felt so thankful to have such thoughtful
friends.
Everything was ready for our baby girl's arrival.
        The night before I went into hospital for
the c-section, I was so busy running about like
a blue arsed fly, cleaning the house, sorting
Billy and Nyla's clothes for the week, at the
same time as sticking notes for Brad
everywhere, that I slipped and fallen arse over

tit, top to bottom down the god damn stairs. Cradling my huge bump, I scrambled up to my feet as if nothing had happened.

The following morning, feeling sick with worry (and a bruised butt) I kissed Nyla and Billy goodbye, saving the tears for in the car. I was a pro at this by now, I just wasn't used to leaving my babies and when I did, I was overcome with emotion. I was the same when they started nursery and school, I'd be walking around behind them wiping my tears, they were oblivious, as for their injections I swear I cried more than they ever did.

I was admitted to the ward and was told that I was due in theatre at 10 am. I was all gowned up and ready to go as I lay on the bed stroking my bump, cherishing the moment that this would be the last time I would feel pregnant. I could feel her squirming about, I wondered what it must have felt like to just be laying there all nice and cosy, minding your own business and then wham … hello world. The consultant came up to see me because my blood pressure and heart rate were high, and they couldn't risk surgery until it had lowered. After an ECG and a few deep breaths, they were happy to go ahead.

On 5 th March 2013, our beautiful baby girl Evelyn was born into the world; she was just beautiful.

I've always believed that she was heaven sent, right from the day she was born she had a real spirit about her, reminding me so much of my beloved Nanna. Nyla and Billy are very much like their dads' side of the family, so it'd be nice to have one take after me, it's only fair right?

Evelyn was born, just one day before Billy's birthday bless him, the C-section was later rescheduled, even though I'm sure Billy wouldn't have minded sharing his birthday with his baby sister.

It had become a running joke that June must have been the favourite month for shagging, as all three of our babies were born within three weeks of each other, despite the years in between them.

I would blush when I got *that* look, when asked their birth dates, not that I cared as I had three beautiful babies, all with the same Pisces star sign which is a true rarity. One year, I thought it would be a wonderful idea to have a huge, shared birthday party for them… big mistake! … *"Erm, my tooths just fell out,"* (as blood is dripping down a child's white party dress) and *"They just hit me,"* *"Someone's blocked the toilet,"* oh and not forgetting, *"Someone's just stuck their finger in the birthday cake."* Aghhhhh never again.

Evelyn grew into such a content and placid baby, Nyla and Billy adored her, especially Billy their bond was so precious, my heart would melt as he kissed her forehead while gently stroking her hair.

I felt happy and positive about the future and hoped that we could finally stick the v up to all the crap that we'd been through and move on. I had settled myself into a routine of coping with life as a mum of three. I'd set my alarm for five am, pour myself a coffee and run a bath. I found by doing this it just gave me that time to mentally prepare myself for the day ahead.

The children's clean clothes would be neatly ironed and laid out the night before, as were their breakfasts so as there was less chaos in the morning. I'd have the dinner prepared and the house clean all before the school run. I was so organised it was unreal.

Evelyn was around six months old when my niece Isla came to stay with us, my sister Holly was struggling with her behaviour, she wasn't getting any support from the school or the doctors, so we came to an agreement that she stay with us for a few days until things settled at home.

We had a close relationship, I just wanted to see her happy so I promised her that I'd do all I could to help her. Weeks had soon turned into months and Isla was still living with us.

I had got myself into a strict routine, I had to really as they were at different schools at opposite ends of the town, Evelyn just went with the flow as she bounced up and down in her pram as we rushed from one place to another. Luckily, the girl's bedroom was big enough to separate in to three sections and worked well, until the odd night here and there, (mainly because Nyla was obsessed with Stevie wonder and Isla liked one direction).

Just before Christmas I had a meeting with the school's liaison officer, she discussed with me how pleased she was with Isla's progress. She also felt that she was now ready to return home, and although it broke my heart, I knew she belonged with her own family.

I sobbed for days after she had gone, we all missed her so much.

As life quietened down again, we decided to have a fresh start, and although we had discussed moving before, it was never the right time, so when the opportunity arose to move, we jumped at it.

The house we were moving to was empty so we were able to move gradually, in fact I moved majority of our old house's contents in our truck, I would just cram whatever I could in and made my way up to the other house. The kiddos soon got used to the odd frying pan or box digging them in the leg after school as we would do another run. They were so excited to move, mostly because of the huge garden that they could run about in.

The house needed a bit of work, nothing major, besides, it would have to wait until we could afford it, especially since I wasn't working now. It was frustrating because I liked to keep a clean and tidy home, which was kind of impossible now with mess everywhere, it played havoc with my OCD. I accepted that it was out of my hands, and I just had to be patient. I had always taught my babies that no matter what happens we must always be thankful that we had a roof over our heads.

I tried so hard to be positive for them, but I knew the same old feelings had returned and I started to worry constantly about everything. I worried about the big shit going on in the world, and I worried about the little shit going on in my own mind. I worried about the school run, I worried about what we're going to have for dinner. I worried about Brad leaving me, and one of my biggest worries was that my babies were growing up too quickly and I hadn't made the most out of every minute with them. I also worried that they didn't love me and thought that I was the worse mum in the world. The list was endless. I dealt with this by completely shutting the world out. The last thing I wanted to do was see anyone or speak to anyone. I just wanted to be left the hell alone. All I wanted to do was light the fire, stay in the warm and potter around the house, thinking about bedtime and that it couldn't come quick enough, because then I knew that I no longer needed to put a front on.

If I could be arsed, I may have a soak in the bath, but often I would end up sitting for hours in the lukewarm water staring into space while biting the hell out of my nails.

I was struggling to keep up with even the easiest of chores around the house. I was suffering with pain from what I thought had been caused by an injury at my clubbersise class, until the pain had started to spread throughout every part of my body. I made an appointment with my doctor, he examined my foot and told me it was planter fasciitis and prescribed pain relief. With my history of addiction, I knew it was risky, but I seriously couldn't cope with the pain. I began to take them daily which led me to slip back into old habits. It didn't matter how much or how strong the pain relief was, the pain wouldn't go. I felt completely useless and depressed, some days I couldn't even walk, it was completely taking over my life.

I found myself yet again sitting in the doctor's surgery, answering the same old questions.

"Do you have little or no interest in doing things?"

"Do you feel you want to harm yourself in any way or end your life?" And there it was, the famous question.

Before answering with a blunt, *"No."* I thought about that question again. My attempt to kill myself would most probably not have ended well, and more than likely I would have survived it. But then in all honesty, I believed that my family would be better off without me, and when I closed my eyes at night, I didn't want to wake up. I just wanted the pain to stop. Hmmm. So, what's the difference?

I left the room, clutching the little green piece of paper, with a prescription for those magic pills.

Life continued to be a constant battle with hospital and doctors' appointments. I was then diagnosed with hypertension. (High blood pressure) Meaning more medication. With heart illness in the family, I didn't think much of it, nor did I realise just how serious it could be.

As the weeks went by, the pain had become unbearable. I felt so exhausted that all I wanted to do was sleep. I noticed that I had a swelling on the side of my neck, and it was getting bigger. My aching body was telling me to take painkillers and go to bed, but my head was shouting at me to get it checked out. After debating, I decided the latter. One minute I was in A and E and the next I was on my way to hospital. At worse I thought it was glandular fever, which was until the doctor came over and told me that if I'd have left it any longer, I probably wouldn't be here, because the swelling was on the inside of my throat which was beginning to block my airways.

I was then dumped on my own in a hospital ward, in an area I wasn't familiar with, I had no phone and no clothes. I tried to shut my eyes, but I couldn't stop worrying. The next morning, they transferred me to a different hospital and prescribed me with antibiotics intravenously for a week. I didn't know how much more my body could stand with them prodding and poking, I just wanted to know what was wrong with me. They kept telling me they didn't know, and when the doctor finally did show, he was hardly full of reassurance. He said that it was a severe infection, he didn't know what had caused it, or if it would return, and with that I was discharged. I was drained with exhaustion from the physical and mental pain. I tried my hardest to suffer in silence, because the last thing I wanted to do was burden those around me. Afterall, I was the one who had a light switch on within me, and I was the one who was overcome by the belief that I had the power to fix everyone else, forgetting that the main person that needed fixing was standing in front of the mirror. I didn't realise that it wasn't my duty to fix everyone and everything, until it was too late. I learnt that some people portray themselves as victims by placing the blame on others, they can't and won't be helped and that wasn't my fault. By the time I learnt of the negative impact this was having on my own health, it had drained the absolute shit out of me.

Everything came to ahead, when one morning I collapsed into a heap on to the floor. Cradling my swollen ankles, while rubbing my feet I began to cry. I knew something wasn't right. I couldn't live like this anymore. I managed to pull myself up and shuffling along the countertop, I managed to hobble into the dining room.

I'd become a shadow of my former self; even worse I'd given up on life.

I sat gazing at the pills neatly laid out in front of me, I just wanted it all to stop.

The voice of hope

An hour had passed, and I am still staring at
the packets of pills.
I had completely lost my way and given up on
all hope, I didn't want to be here in this world
anymore. I had convinced myself that now was
my time to go, I wanted to slip away quietly
into the most peaceful sleep.
The physical and emotional pain had taken
over my tired body.

Wearily, I penned Brads name on an
envelope and laid it on the table. It contained
things I wanted him to tell the children,
especially how much I loved them every day. I
had written lists of chores and things that had
to be done with the children and around the
house, from how to plait hair, to how often the
bedsheets should be changed.
This is what it felt like to hit rock bottom. I
longed to feel someone's arms around me,
reassuring me that everything was going to be
ok, yet all I felt was loneliness.
I'd failed my family, and I'd failed myself.
I walked over to the sink to pour a glass of
water, I waited for a minute for the water to
run cold when something caught my eye

through the smeared glass window. There stood a little robin on the fence, looking right at me. I had this coldness run through my entire body, stopping me in my tracks. I quickly reached for the pills and washed them down the plug hole.

I had pulled myself out of it. That's right … ME, I did this, MYSELF.

Weather that robin was a coincidence or not, I believe he was my little saviour. I knew what I had to do next, so I picked up my phone and googled "mental health helplines." My Nanna volunteered for the Samaritans, so I was familiar with the name that was at the top of the list. There was a phone number and an email address, so I decided to email them.

I completely opened up my heart to them, I told them everything. I started right at the beginning, from the childhood trauma to how I felt that day. I felt like a huge weight had been lifted afterwards.

They replied pretty quickly and suggested that I contact my GP again about my mental health and the pain.

I explained to the GP about the chronic pain over the years and how it was affecting every aspect of my life. He arranged various scans,

X-rays and bloods and referred me to a rheumatologist.

Meet Florrie fibro…

After appointments explaining to different consultants that for years I had suffered with chronic pain, fatigue and well sickness in general. The evidence was clear to them by the amount appointments and clinics I'd been to previously up to when it got worse recently. We discussed how my periods at an early age had also impacted my life, contributing to the pain both mentally and physically. I wanted to have a normal healthy life like my friends, instead I was the emotional, sick friend and I hated that. We also went back to 2004. I was looking forward to celebrating my twenty first birthday, when the pain had come back to slap me in the face. Having finished a busy shift at the hospital, I assumed that how I felt was because I'd been on my feet, so I sat down on the sofa and fell asleep. When I woke up, I felt literally paralysed, my legs were numb, I tried to get up, but my body was lifeless, I'd never felt anything like it. I was stuck there in tears until Brad came home from work. I felt so stupid as he carried me up the stairs to bed.

The pain continued on and off over the years, I just put it down to the manual side of nursing and getting older. I just learnt to fight on like I always had done. It was like we were trying to piece together this complicated puzzle, by going back in time trying to pinpoint where it had all started.

It flared up with each pregnancy. I imagined it was to be expected, when growing a tiny human in my belly. I had learnt the art of painting on a smile and hiding behind my addictions through drink and drugs. It was easier to do that because I'd had such negative experiences with doctors and hospitals over the years, plus I didn't want to keep bothering them with my complaining when there were others worse than I was.

Over the next few months, I had further tests done for conditions such as arthritis, due to my swelling feet, ankles, and joint pain. Eventually I was referred to another consultant, Dr Tailby who was fantastic. She conducted the most thorough examinations explaining exactly what she was looking for. For the first time someone was listening to me. Within a couple of weeks, I was back to see Dr Tailby for my results. I sat in the waiting room, praying for answers. After examining me again and checking my body for tender points, which was excruciating. Dr Tailby then sat down with me, showing me diagrams of the body and went through each test that had been carried out and the results of them. She then proceeded to diagnose me with fibromyalgia. Fibro what?? I just sat in silence and stared at her blankly for a moment. Dr Tailby talked to me a little about the condition and explained that it causes widespread chronic pain throughout the body, resulting in sleep problems, fatigue, and even emotional distress. I asked what had caused it, and more importantly how could I stop it. unfortunately, she told me that at present there no cure for what I had, and it was just going to be a case of managing it with medications, advising me also to avoid as much stress as I could, to prevent flare ups. She wrote me a prescription for some medication to treat the chronic pain. I couldn't thank Dr Tailby enough for her kindness and reassurance, after years and years of living with the unknown I finally had some answers, for which was all I could have hoped. Dr Tailby passed me a tissue to wipe my eyes, it was just a relief to finally be believed. Before I left, she handed me an information booklet, assuring me that now I was diagnosed all I had to do was ring and request an appointment if I had any concerns.

My head was spinning, trying to make sense of everything. I spent hours researching causes as well as self-help. One thing I did discover, was that fibromyalgia can stem from trauma of all kinds. It was all starting to make sense now. However, Fibromyalgia can be so misunderstood for several reasons, and it's not always possible to be diagnosed. When I told friends and family I would receive mixed responses, some understood and others suggested that it was a cop out for not knowing what was wrong with me, suggesting it was all in my head. I didn't need anyone else's opinions, this pain was real, and I wouldn't wish it upon anyone. Fibromyalgia had already stolen so much of my life, and I was determined that I wasn't going to let it win.

After a month or so of coping as best as I could with the pain and the meds, I had another big flare up. I was in agony and exhausted. In fact, the fatigue was so bad I just wanted to sleep whenever I could. I made an appointment to see the rheumatologist which I was soon to regret it. My consultant was on leave, so it was a registrar that I saw. I immediately got the impression that I was wasting his time, because he was so unbelievably rude. He told me to go home, get some sleep and rest and accept that this is my life now. To add insult to injury he then added that it was never going to get any better. I must also try to lose weight and exercise. Did he know how it felt to be on a hamster wheel of pain… exercise. pain…exercise. obviously not. I felt like I had been slapped in the face. So, it was all in my head then, right?

From then on, I suffered in silence popping pills daily. He was right I had to accept I was never going to be the same again.

I'd wake up feeling ninety. I couldn't eat, I couldn't sleep, I couldn't function, I had my meds changed a lot. I was so fed up. I felt like no one believed the pain I was in just because it wasn't visible, I just always felt like I was moaning and let us face it no one likes a moaning myrtle.

I sat in the hospital waiting for blood tests, thoughts came back to when I was nine years old when this all started, I was so fed up with it. I didn't want to keep putting myself through appointments and clinics I just had to try and help myself as best as I could. I decided from that day that it is what it is. I call her Florrie Fibro and she's a part of me, but she doesn't define me. I'd just be grateful for what I could do when I could do it. If it was a good day yay! If it was a difficult day soak in bath and pjs on and lots of self-care.

Meet Betty bipolar…
As with any physical pain comes emotional pain and sometimes depression. It all goes hand in hand. (Or maybe not and I'm just proper greedy) Although I would say my mental health issues started long before the physical pain did.

I was always a very nervous child, a real worrier, I worried about everyone and every little thing, I worried until it made me sick. I would bite my nails until they bled from the age of four.

No one knew about the abuse, but I would say I felt anxious even before that. Maybe that is why he chose me. I don't know.

One of my therapists once said that I had an antenna for atmospheres, I knew straight away if someone had a had an argument, I could even feel if one was brewing around me. I was always trying to work people out in my head. How they looked, how they dressed how they smelt.

As I grew up, I learned to understand I was highly sensitive, this was also very negative part of my personality.

I was so emotional, especially at occasions, not attention crying but sad crying, because it was over. I didn't like things to be finished because it would fill me with emptiness and sadness, but I didn't understand why. I would get so overwhelmed at Christmas and birthdays that I'd hide when friends and family had to leave. I would hug my grandparents so tight, Nanna would say "come on sunbeam don't cry" as she gently rubbed my hand bless her gorgeous heart. I felt safe and loved and wanted to hang on to every second of it.

So, overall growing up I knew I was a bit different if you like.

By the time I was at high school and boys came along my emotions were running wild and my heart felt many breaks too, and to me it was exactly that. A broken heart that could not be fixed. Sobbing into my pillow hurting, feeling so rejected I then jumped from boy to boy to boy I just wanted to feel loved so got used to all the heart ache as I went along. I was never without a boyfriend right up until leaving school as I just craved for that love and attention no matter how small.

In all seriousness though My emotions really were taking over I cried daily I felt so down and low about myself I wanted to hurt myself all the time I wanted it to all go away. As mentioned before my Mum had enough and demanded I see a doctor.
After writing down how I felt, thinking it would help the doctor understand. Sniggering that it was my personality, wasn't the exact response I had expected. He made me feel like shit.

As I got older, I found that Some days were better than others, my moods were completely off the scale with feeling so high one day that I could fix the world and everyone in it to then feeling so low that I wanted to die.

The highs were fabulous, especially when I was spending money on crap that I didn't need. I would sit up in the middle of the night and order one hundred toothbrushes on Amazon, forgetting about it until they arrived. I'd stockpile hundreds of tubes of toothpaste, shaving gel, air fresheners and lotions. It's like I had a huge fear of running out of something. (Mind you it has helped in lock down) So I'd feel great for a while but as always with the highs came the lows, and the lows were the worst, refusing to look after myself. I'd shut myself away from the outside world. I'd would sit on the edge of the bed every morning and swallow a handful of meds.

I felt utterly burnt out and one particular week I was so unstable and emotional. When I felt like this id make rash decisions and this time, I thought it'd be a clever idea to come off all my meds. I made an appointment with a nurse practitioner for the same day. Once I got in there, I burst into tears. I told her said I'd that I'd had enough of life and meds, she agreed for me to just stop taking them. She never advised me on how to gradually come off them or anything, so I stopped taking them and imagined I'd feel better in a few days. Two days later I began to shake uncontrollably and started throwing up. I took a deep breath and walked into the kitchen to start the dinner because no matter how I have felt Ive always tried to protect my children from it, to be honest they are oblivious most of the time as they are too busy playing together.

One evening I was on my way to see my friend Clara to have my nails done when A strange feeling washed over me, and I couldn't shake off those dark emotions. Clara was one of my closest friends and often she'd have poured me a glass of rose before I'd arrived. What I loved most is that with Clara I didn't need have to put a brave fave on. We always had so much to chat about, but I felt like I was completely on another planet this particular night. Clara knew something was wrong, so I just blurted it out. I told her how I'd felt so suicidal again and didn't know what to do. First, she wrapped me up in a huge hug with tears in her eyes. She assured me that I was far from weak just because I needed to take medication to feel better. She told me that she was going to make a phone call to my doctor and demand he see me I pleaded with her not to, but then it was nearly six o'clock so id imagine they would be closed so I agreed. I heard Clara say to she was worried for my safety. it made me feel sick and embarrassed but also it made me realise I also needed help now. The doctor was going to call me the next morning.

I am so thankful to my friend for that night because I don't know what I would have done without her. I went home feeling mentally drained and physically exhausted.

The next morning, I ran a bath and at dead on 8 am my mobile rang with a withheld number, I was so surprised the doctor had remembered me.

I will never forget my conversation with that doctor. He was the most understanding doctor to which I had ever spoken. I explained to him what had happened and that I was struggling so badly especially since the fibromyalgia diagnosis I said it felt like my world fell apart. I told him that it felt like I was grieving for the person that I was not anymore and that it hurt so badly. Not once did he rush me, he admitted that what the nurse practitioner did was wrong, and she should never have advised me to just stop taking any medication.

Reassuringly he told me that he was going to take the matter further. He said that I should continue to take my medication and go back up to the double dose I was on previously. I asked him *"when will I ever come off them?"* pausing he then replied, *"when you're feeling 90% better"*

"And what if I'm never that?" I asked. *"Listen, there is no right or wrong answers, and it really doesn't matter if you have to take them for the rest of your life. so be it"* he answered in a caring way. The doctor also told me that he imagined the pressure had got too much for me and I had suffered from some kind of breakdown. He convinced me to agree to CBT and therapy sessions, because he thought they'd be beneficial to me. I felt calmer after my phone call with him because of his caring nature probably and I could see more clearly now. Sometimes you need to hit rock bottom to realise that the only way is up.

My instincts told me that it was the right thing to take my meds, just every now and again I would have a blip when my head would get involved and I'd forget about my strengths and I'd solely focus on my mistakes, instead of remembering that everyone makes them and that's ok.

I then made a promise to myself that I would do whatever it takes to fight this I would attend every type of therapy there was available to me.

The first therapist I saw dealt with mostly anxiety, so after explaining to her about the past, she was honest with me from the start and said it was a specialist type of therapy I needed. which was fine I had to explore every avenue possible. I was then referred to another therapist who I didn't get on with, we just didn't gel, and she was really patronising. I gave it five weeks and then cancelled the future appointments. Lauryn was the last therapist I saw, she was lovely. She was a lot younger than me, and I didn't feel she couldn't understand certain situations, through no fault of her own. I saw her for about a year and we did work on self-help and other coping strategies.

After a year I think we both thought that the therapy would have had a more positive outcome than it had. On one of our last sessions, we discussed further support because of how up and down I was still feeling. Lauryn asked for my permission to conduct a further assessment as she believed I may have bipolar disorder, in which case id need to be referred to a psychiatrist. That literally scared the hell out of me. not something else I thought.

To be honest by now it didn't come as a shock to me, because it had been suggested in the past when I was younger, it just was never investigated further. The results came back as high, indicating that it was highly likely. I was referred to my doctor as I needed to be under the care of the psychiatrists. The waiting list was around four months and when I met the psychiatrist Richie, he was so understanding. He was supportive and had a calm way of explaining the disorder. (Although I did tend to just let information go in one ear and out the other, as I nodded and shook my head I always find when I am having to listen, especially when its essential information, my mind completely shuts off and I start thinking of the most random shit.)

We discussed moving forward with medications and explained which combination of psychiatric drugs worked better alongside each other. I just had to be prepared for rocky few weeks as they were inevitably going to be challenging.

As predicted, it took a while to experiment with different meds that worked. The first one I gained a stone in four weeks, I was mortified! Considering that my weight was one of the biggest reasons that impacted my mental health, I knew this wasn't good for me mentally and physically.

After Richie suggesting I try just one more combination, I hesitantly agreed. I knew this wasn't an overnight fix, it was going to take time and patience.

The new combination of medication was by far the best decision, and I didn't look back.

Yes, I have continued with my ups and downs, but they are much more manageable. However, I did feel that Doctors had signed me off at that point, but do you know what? "Bipolar disorder," "fibromyalgia," they are just names, who cares if you have that label? No one that matters in your life anyway, at the end of the day they are part of who I am, which is why I named them "Florrie fibromyalgia" and "betty bipolar" and I've learnt to both accept and even laugh about them some days, which is what gets me through the tough times.

I know that there is no cure for my illness, but it's how I chose to deal with it that matters, remembering that just because one day may be a bad day doesn't mean it's a bad life. I was thankful that I was finally able to understand the reasons why I felt like I did and cope with it to the best of my ability.

I began to realise that life was too short and precious to waste. I just had to look at the bigger picture and be thankful for the blessings that I had in my life and focus on what I could do ad not what I wasn't able to.
  I didn't realise that my strength had been there all along, I just had to search a little deeper for it that was
        I had given Brad chance after chance to leave me, I would tell him he deserved so much better than me. The truth was I wanted to save him so badly and set him free of my complicated world. He didn't understand any of it and in his defence how could he comprehend something you have never experienced? He is also a 'fixer' the trouble was this couldn't be solved with a bar of chocolate and that frustrated him and would lead him to

withdraw from me. I'm just so grateful to him for sticking by my side and not giving up on me.

I did find it sad that I had thought so little of myself that I'd allow myself to be used and abused because I just wanted to feel wanted and liked. In fact, it breaks my heart that I've spent over 30 years of being a people pleaser. I'd come to understand though there's a balance between being people pleaser and caring for others. When I was growing up, I would spend my birthday and Christmas money on family and friends on gifts to show them I loved them, that's just my nature and it always will be. I love sending little gifts and cards to the special people in my life (who know who they are and may even be reading this, I love you x) I just want them to know how special they are to me and how thankful I am to have them in my life, the difference is I know those close to me appreciate it.

I love to buy presents and nice clothes for Brad and the kiddos, while I live in my legging's, baggy t-shirts or jammys with holes in. That's just who I am.

I am ME… and that's enough

"Hi, my lovely", I called to my friend Louise as I excitedly opened the door to her quaint little shop. I was so proud of her for opening her very own place in our small village. Breathing in the calmness, and the sweet smell of incense that hung in the air, I walked around the shop. I gazed at the beautiful *yankee candles*, and *willow tree* figurines on display.

"You're not yourself, come on let's have a cuppa and catch up." Louise always knew when I wasn't right. *"To be honest I feel like I'm lost, its like I'm searching for something that's missing, but I don't know what it is, if that makes sense."* I confided in her. Louise was one of the few friends that I had, that just 'got me,' so I knew she'd understand. After our little heart to heart, I had another wonder around the shop,

admiring the beautiful crystals, when I felt drawn to a pack of purple angel oracle cards. I asked Louise what they were, she explained that they were used to bring comforting messages from angels and loved ones. I had like a strange, warm feeling inside, so I instinctively bought them.

Once home, I took the large shiny cards with their gold rim out of the packet, I then carefully shuffled them. I had a question on my mind, eager for a message. I turned over the first card, *"There's nothing to worry about."*

A shiver ran down my spine when it occurred to me what I'd asked, *"Is everything going to be okay?"*

I couldn't believe my eyes, there was forty-four different cards, and that was the one to come through for me. The more I used them, the more my confidence grew, and I started to feel more positive about my life, and my future became much clearer. Every morning I'd sit quietly and read my cards, which never ceased to amaze me. I'll be forever grateful to Louise, she is a beautiful soul who helped me find myself, after years of feeling so lost.

I went on to join different spiritual circles to channel my energy, until I found one, I felt comfortable and settled in. Finding my faith in Spiritualism became an important part of my journey to healing. The friends and family that mattered to me supported me, (I think others just thought I was an absolute nutter), not because they understood it, but because they saw a change in me. I was out for dinner with my friend one night when I was telling her all about it, she told me that she wasn't surprised. She went on to tell me that she was spiritual herself, and there was something she'd always wanted to tell me. *"Do you remember when we both worked at the hospital? Well, I was walking down the corridor one day and you were waiting near the reception, as I got closer, I saw this bright light surrounding you."* I felt so emotional because I knew exactly when she meant, I was expecting Nyla. I wasn't freaked out about it at all, it was more of a comfort.

I began to research holistic methods for healing, trauma, and physical pain. I was curious to what alternatives there were, as a pose to medications. I came across Reiki healing and decided to go ahead and study it.

Reiki is an energy healing technique that promotes relaxation, reduces stress and anxiety, through gentle touch. Reiki can also support the wellbeing of those receiving traditional medical treatments such as chemotherapy, radiation and general surgery. I found it so amazing that after months of challenging work and dedication, I became a qualified Reiki practitioner.

Times were hard when I started up my own business from home, my best friend Kerry had just given up as a beauty therapist to complete her nursing degree. Kerry gave me her portable treatment bed, bless her heart, she was such a good friend. I was able to make up a calm area in the house with incense, candles, and a little music player. I found that by practicing Reiki it filled that gap of nursing, and the interaction with patients that I missed. It was a little slow to start with, but I pushed the self-doubt to the back of my mind, stayed positive and eventually it picked up and I was seeing regular clients.

I couldn't believe how popular it had become, when I started to receive invites for events and parties. I felt so blessed that I was able to give comfort and healing to those who needed it most. The sceptics never bothered me either, that's how I knew that this was the right path for me. I felt unstoppable when I learned about the law of attraction and manifestation, based on the belief that thoughts are a form of energy, with positive energy attracting success in all areas of life. The more I focused on this, I found myself protected from negative and toxic people and situations.

The next life changing event that contributed to my healing process, was discovering hypnotherapy. I wouldn't normally read leaflets that come through the letter box, but I'm so glad I did that day.

I flicked through the booklet full of adverts for plumbers, electricians, and various health therapies, when an advert jumped out to me, '*Forever living hypnotherapy.*' I remember years back my Nanna trying to convince my Mam to have it, because she honestly believed it worked. What had I got to lose? I messaged the lady for more information in the hope of booking an appointment, her friendly positive energy put me at ease right away. I can hand on heart tell you that from that very first session, something changed within me for the better. I continued to see her on a weekly basis, and we became good friends. I hope she reads this, because I want her to know how thankful I am to her. What she taught me will stay with me always. I would look for the positives in every aspect of life, no matter how hard I had to search I could always find one. While at the same time the heaviness began to lift, leaving me feeling restful and calm. I could see life in a different light altogether, realising that things were never as bad as they seemed. I learnt to accept that life was all about give and take, and that it was ok to use the word, "no," without feeling the guilt.

It was the wakeup call I needed to have, hit rock bottom, break down, cry and be torn apart, to prove that I will always find the strength within, to pick myself up, and put myself back together. I have discovered the importance of putting my own needs first, and that the path that leads to happiness and success is never going to be easy. I've had to experience the tough times, to recognise and appreciate the better ones. It starts with small goals such as, getting up every morning, opening the windows to let in the fresh air, making the beds and getting dressed. Being organised helps me to feel in control, it gives me the confidence to achieve realistic goals.

Ok so my home isn't as immaculate as it was before, and I haven't completed the long list of chores, but hey I've accomplished three of them, and when I go to bed at night, I can feel proud of myself.

As I moved along in my healing journey towards freedom, I discovered that life and success is all about the mindset. If you're not in the right frame of mind, everything you do becomes a challenge. It wasn't until I practised mindfulness that I understood the power of it. Let's face it, does a boxer go into the ring chanting, *"I'm not going to win, I'm not going to do this, I'm not good enough…?"* Well, none that I've ever known anyway, especially not Tyson Fury.

Pushing myself to limits that I knew I couldn't reach would just lead to exhaustion, so instead I poured my energy into writing a journal every day, dedicating just a few minutes to write and focus on self-love. I found various activities that I could practise and improve my relationship with myself. I began to feel the pressures of life becoming less and less. I finally felt in control, even on the difficult days. When I was struggling, instead of being a mardy pants, I'd do something for myself. I knew both my body and mind would thank me for it. I'd let go of my worries and give myself time to recharge my batteries. I practised meditation and yoga, feeling stronger with each session I did. Once I'd found my peace, I made a promise to myself that I'd no longer allow others to hold power over me. It was my life, to live my way. Thinking positively has enabled me to let go of my negative thought pattern and realise that no matter how much I try, I can't change anyone, but neither should I judge them, as I'm ashamed to say I have in the past. We live in an ignorant world, and we don't stop to notice the battles that others are quietly fighting alone. I'll always do my best to reach out to others and show kindness and compassion, because I've been there. There's a difference in being there for someone and being used by someone, and I know now that if the behaviour of others is affecting my life in a negative way, protecting my self is paramount.

If you take nothing else from this, listen up and remember ... never believe all you see on social media, you're only shown what people choose to display to you, let's be honest come on, who's going to take you with them while they take a crap, or parade around outside while putting the trash out with their hair in a messy bun, (probably me, actually.) They don't want to show you the original unfiltered photo they just took, that may I add is way more beautiful. It's a sad world we live in, and it's our job to make a difference. We need to encourage others to find the strength to believe in themselves and be proud of who they are. Strength can be found in many ways. It could be a friend, or someone close to you that you feel you can share absolutely anything with, (and I mean absolutely anything!) To help you through your darkest days. I know on one hand who I can reach out to when I'm struggling, and they will one million percent be there and vice versa. It doesn't matter who it is, whether it be a councillor, therapist or professional you can share your thoughts with, just trust and have faith that they will help you. I can promise you that you will find that someone. I always say to anyone, my inbox is always open, and I mean it so please don't ever feel alone, because a problem shared is a problem halved.

So, find your 'how' and discover your 'why.'

It feels so much better to laugh and look for the positives in life rather than focus on the negative, life is way too precious for that.

So put the kettle on make yourself a brew and just ...... breathe.

I'd been contemplating how to end my book for a while, the main reason for this is, I want to leave a positive message to all of you. However, I chose not to sugar coat it in the slightest. That's not real-life peeps, and we know it, right? The truth is I don't want to give you the impression that my life is now as rosy as ever. My life will never be even close to perfect, and well … is anyone's? I'll most probably be on psychiatric meds until I take my last breath, and I may do the odd thing here and there that maybe I shouldn't, but do you know what? that's ok. None of this has been easy and there have been times when I have seriously regretted telling my story, I then remind myself of why I did it and I feel proud for finding the strength within me to speak my truth.

Today I am a Mama, wife, daughter, sister, and friend but most important of all…

I AM ME.

A few final words with love from me to you x

March 2020 and coronavirus had descended on the whole entire world, bringing with it the most tragic events. I also lost my biggest love and hero, my precious Dad, which affected my life tremendously.

It leaves me questioning what means most to me.

The simple things in life for sure, gratitude and the positive impact of learning to love and appreciate ourselves, while taking the time to look at the world around us, capturing its beauty that I for one had never even stopped to notice before. The sun, the moon, and the stars, notice how brightly they shine. So simple, yet so needed in this uncertain world in which we are living in right here, right now.

You may think that you don't matter in this world, but because of you, just remember this, someone is drinking out of their favourite mug that YOU bought them. Someone is listening that one song on the radio that reminds them of YOU. Someone has just remembered something funny YOU said, and YOU made them laugh.

Never ever think that you don't have an impact on someone else's life. Your fingerprints can't be wiped away from the little marks of kindness that only YOU have left behind.

Never give up hope that there will always be a brighter tomorrow.

Love always x

Let the past go and let all things unloving fall away,

Keep the lessons and the love but forget the rest, and just learn from it,

See the love within yourself and those around you.

My fave self-love rituals are,

- Light a scented candle, run a hot bath, and pour in relaxing oils or salts or a bath bomb

- Face mask and facial massage with essential oils (using a you tube video)

- Calming yoga

- Giving yourself a manicure or pedicure

- Mug of something hot, (it feels like a big hug.)

Self-love journaling

First, inhale the 'new' and exhale the 'old'

- Gratitude - list three things that you are grateful for, by counting your blessings every day helps you to feel more positive instantly.

It may be that you give thanks for your home, a family member, a friend, the blue sky, the moon, or the stars, absolutely anything you feel grateful for.

- Kindness - how have you spoken to yourself today? Have you been too hard on yourself? Write down three positive things about you.

- Happiness - list three things that make you happy

- Declutter - I love this one! there's nothing like a good old session of chucking out any crap that you've been holding onto for absolutely no reason at all. Throw away any thing that you feel is weighing you down, for example, old paperwork, receipts or simply sort out your handbag or a drawer even (we all have that one junk drawer) it's amazing how much better you will feel.

- Meditate – if you are unsure check out you tube or apps there are free ones. Dedicate just five minutes out of your day, to quieten your mind and switch off from the outside world, if you struggle to relax then just use the five minutes to close your eyes and practise deep breathing.

- Move – removing tension from your body is a must, for as little or as often as you're able, yoga, aerobics, even a boogie around to music as you do the housework. (Much to my kiddos annoyance) Focus on the positives- list three qualities you have

- Treat yourself to a bunch of flowers … just because

- Pay someone a compliment or send a thoughtful message to a friend or family

member to show them that they are
loved

- Lists – plan a manageable daily routine
  for example, three meals a day, exercise,
  make the bed

- Unfollow- unfollow and block any social
  media accounts that do nothing for you

- Love- say the words 'I love you' to
  yourself, I know it sounds insane but if
  you're like me and you send your love so
  freely to the special people in your life,
  what's the difference? YOU MATTER

- Find fun- having a laugh is so important, watch something funny, have dance around to some old tunes and have a good old sing along. Life is such a wheel of emotions that it's so important to get off every now and again and have fun

- Digital detox- yep ditch the gram for 24 hours or if that's too harsh give yourself a time limit before bed, my phone is set where all the apps turn off at 8 pm and turn on again at 8 am otherwise you find your phone owns you not the other way around.

- Drink two litres of water to improve your mood, filling a bottle the night before can help.

- Joy – wear something that makes YOU happy, your fave colour, outfit, earrings, mascara lippy or perfume.

- Do something kind for yourself

- Forgive yourself for any mistakes in the past and let them go.

- Another thing that really helped me was to write myself a letter as though writing to your best friend. I did one to my younger self, but you can write a letter to your former self, either way its such a healing way of coming to terms with trauma and painful events. Remember to talk kind to yourself with compassion, love and patience.

- Allow yourself to daydream.

- Write a bucket list.

Finally, I would just like to give thanks to whoever has taken the time to read my story and congratulate you if you've made it to the end! I hope you can take some comfort from it by feeling reassured that you are never alone. Remember that there's never a right or wrong way to talk about how we are feeling, it's that first conversation that is the most important one that we have.

Try not to put too much pressure on yourself and open up as often as you feel able to.

focus on each day at a time and avoid putting extra pressure on yourself, you're doing just fine.

Visualise the life that you want and chose the path that brings you the most happiness.

MAKE IT HAPPEN!

Thank you again so much, sending you a whole lot of love and hope for a brighter future, you've got this.

My inbox is always open, and I will do my upmost to answer as soon as I'm able to.

Beckycraig1012@icloud.com

Tik-tok; bex1012xx
Instagram; bex1012xx

There are many confidential mental health services, I've listed some contacts that I have found to be of great comfort in my darkest times. Most of these services offer 24-hour emotional support for those who need to talk.

NHS 111
www.connectin
gwithpeople.org
www.changingminds.co.uk

Mind
Mental health   03001233393
Email   Info@mind.org.uk
Text   86436

Samaritans
116123
Samaritans.org
Email jo@samaritans.org

Papyrus helpline uk
0800 068 41 41
Text 07786209697
Papyrus-org.uk

The survivors trust
08088 010818

C.A.L.L
Community advice and listening line
0800132373
Text 81066
HELP plus message

The mix
08088084994
Text 85258
Text THE MIX

●

Rethink mental illness
0300 5000927
Rethink.org

Women's aid   08451232311

Cruse bereavement care
0808 808 1677
Cruse.org.uk

NSPCC
0808 800 5000

Domestic abuse helpline 24 hr
0808 2000 247

Acknowledgements

Thank you to my incredible family and friends who have been behind me all the way on this journey. You've wiped away my tears, kicked me up the arse and encouraged me to carry on until the end. I never imagined that I'd be able to self-publish a book, but with thanks to my special friend who kindly edited throughout, you've made it possible. I'm forever in your debt.

Finally, I thank you my reader, bless you all.

Printed in Great Britain
by Amazon

22595077R00215